Inviting the Queen

An Emerging Archetype for Women at Midlife

A PERSONAL GUIDEBOOK

Sandra Rogers, MA, LMFT

ISBN: 978-1-950186-12-9

Cover and interior design by Jennifer Leigh Selig
(www.jenniferleighselig.com)

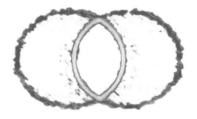

MANDORLA BOOKS
WWW.MANDORLABOOKS.COM

DEDICATION

I dedicate this book to my husband, Larry Ansley,
a king among men, who lived with its writing,
and made room in his life for a wife
who was in gestation mode for five years.

And to my dear friend, Patricia Ariadne, Ph.D.,
who was a dedicated godmother,
encouraging and helping me realize that I could
write and publish this book.

TABLE OF CONTENTS

INTRODUCTION:

INVITING THE QUEEN

You have just seen your last child off to college, or you have just turned the books of your business over to the new owner. Or perhaps another kind of event is taking place that is signaling to you that a major phase of your life is receding in your rearview mirror. You may have looked forward to this day for a long time, and in particular to having "nothing to do" and "no one to answer to." But now that the day has come, instead of feeling the sense of accomplishment you expected, you think: "What now?"

You imagine you have many more years of life ahead, and, of course, you have made plans for them, but something is missing. Even more on your mind than "What now?" is the question "Who am I?"

Who are you now that you are no longer primarily the nurturer in your family? Who are you now that you are no longer a senior project manager at the architectural firm you helped put on the map? The list can go on and on.

If you are looking for active female role models for this new life phase, you may be learning that they are few and far between. You know you are not ready just to play doting grandmother or become a lady who lunches. You have a lot of energy and vitality left in you, not to mention the wisdom of a lifetime of valuable experiences and skills to share. What will you do and who you shall be for the next several years—possibly even decades—until either your health or energy diminish, signaling a time to slow down and recede more into yourself, is an important decision.

Perhaps you will decide that the next stage of your life is to be lived within the framework of the Queen archetype. If so, you may decide that you are ready and willing to invite the Queen. That is what this book is intended to help you decide.

I use the word *decide* here with great intention, because inviting the Queen might not be of interest to every woman. It is a conscious decision. Although the Queen archetype exists in potential for every woman, not every woman will want to invite her energy in when she reaches midlife. Claiming the potent energy of the Queen for our own is heady stuff, and like all good things, it requires a bit of stretching,

In modern neo-paganism as influenced by Robert Graves's writings, the Triple Goddess is thought to represent the three stages of a woman's life and are referred to as the Maiden, the Mother, and the Crone. The Maiden is an unmarried, chaste, also naïve and unschooled woman, who is pure feminine potential. The Mother is a woman who is sexual and procreative; she's producing the next generation—of humans, and in parallel, also of creations. The Crone is a woman whose mothering duties are complete. Although she is wise and may serve as an historian for her people, as the keeper of the community's traditions, she is going into a more introspective life phase.

But the world has changed, and women's roles are no longer defined as they once were. We women live longer and hold professional roles outside our homes, and we feel relevant and productive in our lives for decades longer than our forebears did. The Queen is not a new archetype. She has appeared many times and represents the highest form of the feminine. With that being said, it seems to me that "Queen" is the proper name for this life stage and archetype in this new Quaternity between Mother and Crone. She represents a woman in full awareness of herself who is contributing to her family and a wider community. Like a Mother, but with a broader perspective, she is a leader and a visionary.

To Invite the Queen is to become more aware of and seek the energy of the Queen archetype within yourself, interpreting the meaning of this in the light of who you are, and then opening to allow this concept to become more fully embodied within you. With practice, you may draw considerable strength from the imagery of the Queen and experience yourself as powerful and wise—and certainly not as someone who is feeble or ready to retreat.

We women integrate and take on the role of the Mother when we first become the bearers and nurturers of children or other entities, such as businesses or creative projects. We spend time considering this identity, seeking information on what it means to be a Mother, and as we become more filled with information and knowledge, the archetypal energy takes hold of us and finds a home in our psyches. In part, this happens in the realm of the *collective unconscious*, as psychologist Carl Jung called it. The collective unconscious is the universal dimension of the psyche, and thus, a psychological opening to the Mother archetype comes to all women who feel drawn to the growing or nurturing aspects of life. In addition, much of the information related to this archetype and our beliefs about the role of the Mother is handed down to us through our family and culture. Some of the information we internalize about the Mother is learned in conventional ways, such as through books and courses, as well as our discussions with friends and family. Ultimately, it is primarily a woman's own choice of turning toward it that causes the energy of the Mother archetype to enter her life and be expressed in some manner through her.

It is also so with the archetype of the Queen. The difference is that, historically, the Queen did not have a place in most women's lives—for a very simple reason: Most women did not live long enough!

Until the beginning of the twentieth century, most women bore and raised their children, took care of their homes and husbands, perhaps entered menopause (if they survived long enough), and then died. Within the last 100 years we have seen many more women survive childbirth and other diseases like tuberculosis and cancer, and live much longer than their predecessors.

This longer time, perhaps as much as thirty years would be a long time to find ourselves living within the archetype of the wise old woman, or Crone. Most of us are not ready to give up the more youthful and vigorous energy associated with the Mother in our fifties and sixties—or even our seventies and eighties, if we remain healthy. Even if we have some gray in our hair and weigh a bit more than we did in our youth, women are playing roles in society, as businesspeople, as politicians, and as leaders and matriarchs. Unless we are ill, our minds work well and we see things clearly. What are we to do with all the energy and vigor we still have and the experience we have accrued thus far if not participate and continue to build with it? It would not be a good use of resources for educated, experienced, and vital women who, for the most part, are still engaged with the outer world to move too quickly into the more introverted, interior world that the Crone archetype has so traditionally held as its domain.

It is appropriate for women in midlife to respectfully salute the Crone, knowing that her archetypal energy is waiting for us, but that it is not yet time to invite her in. Instead, we should issue a timelier invitation to the archetype of the Queen, asking her to help us feel her energy within us so we may get to know the gifts and fresh energy she can bring to our recently expanded life stages and social roles.

That is what this book is about!

How to Use This Book

Inviting the Queen is divided into two parts. Part One, "Archetypes Women Embody," is theoretical: It explains the key concepts of archetypes, how they work in our psychological lives, and how they might correlate with developmental stages. It will be important to read this first part, so that you have an understanding of how all the many concepts used in this book work together. Fully understanding where and how this newly emerging archetypal energy originated will help you find your inner Queen.

In Part Two, "How to Embody the Queen," we shall explore the Queen archetype through the lens of the chakra system and the qualities of energy and consciousness this archetype contributes to our lives as women. The chakra system is an ancient Hindu system that locates and explores the types and qualities of energy located in the seven energy centers of our bodies. Additionally, other methods of self-exploration, such as meditation, journal writing, and visualization, will be offered to help you invite the Queen archetype into your life and optimize her influence in your behavior and thinking at the elevated level she brings.

PART ONE:

ARCHETYPES WOMEN EMBODY

For those not already familiar with them, understanding the concept of archetypes can seem challenging. An archetype is a recurrent motif found in mythology or literature. Where this gets interesting is that these symbols recur because they have psychological value to the collective imagination. To further your understanding of archetypes, I have used the myths of ancient Greek goddesses, whom the ancient Greeks saw as personifications of archetypal qualities like wisdom and beauty, to describe three archetypal stages in a woman's life. I also have used stories from our contemporary culture to amplify and illustrate those same archetypal energies.

Chapter Two examines the history of women and power. I have included sections in this chapter on internalized misogyny (how women participate in subordinating themselves and other women), the shadow queen in the patriarchy, and as seen in popular culture (also mentioning the work women must do at midlife to integrate their rejected/neglected shadow aspects and embody the Queen). It concludes with what is basically a challenge to those who feel called by the Queen archetype.

The only way you will become a Queen in your own life is first to do the inner work that a Queen needs to do. Become clear about your problems and your strengths and work to change the problematic beliefs and circumstances to foster your own awareness and clarity. Once you have cultivated your vision of how you want your life to be, then comes the work to bring the energy of the Queen in. In other words, once you have recognized the archetype and have seen how the Queen potentially could manifest in your life, it's time to issue the invitation."

CHAPTER 1

AN EMERGING ARCHETYPE FOR WOMEN AT MIDLIFE

There are more women in the Western world aged fifty-five-plus than there have ever been before. We are living longer, healthier lives. We are better educated than our mothers and grandmothers. And because we belong to the first few generations who have aged so well, we have a surprising lack of role models to guide us and help us measure our lives as older women. Aging used to be viewed as a curse—and to be fair, there are women who still view it as such and bemoan every sign of aging. Many of the characteristic roles women used to play which formerly would have served as signposts for us in the past either no longer exist or are perceived as hopelessly outdated stereotypes. We may be biological grandmothers, but most of us don't live grandmotherly lives, as the culture thinks of them. We may be successful in business or academia, but ideas of what that looks like beyond retirement age in corporations or for entrepreneurs who are their own bosses are not clearly defined. There does not seem to be an overarching vision for what is possible for women when they are no longer living within the Mother archetype. Psychologically, we need something to admire in ourselves that accurately depicts our extraordinary depth and humanity.

Women of the baby boom generation, who were born between 1946 and 1962, as a group have challenged and transformed every life stage as they encountered it. Along with our male counterparts, we ushered in the sexual revolution, brought music to a new level of cultural relevancy, tried and often adopted new forms of relationship, ultimately redefining what the term *family* means. Now, having reached midlife, and for some, old age, we have found that the old developmental labels of later life no longer fit.

Although we may no longer be actively involved in playing mothering roles, we are not ready to find the nearest rocking chair and take up knitting full-time either—unless we take pleasure and fulfillment from knitting!

Archetypal psychologists have often borrowed the names of the developmental stages of a woman's life from the pagan concept of the Triple Goddess—Maiden, Mother, and Crone—which has also been denoted as the fertility cycle. For a long time, this seemed to fit women well. Now, it doesn't. Today we live so much longer than our foremothers that there is a much longer period between menopause and the end of life, up to thirty years on average. It seems to most vital women when presented with the image of the Crone, that the Crone is someone much closer to the end of her life than they are.

The inaccurate matching of the Crone archetype to real-life women's activities and self-interests, coupled with the resistance of midlife women to seeing ourselves as fitting into a degenerative developmental phase that ends with us toes up in a coffin, is calling forth a new archetype that is more relevant to a powerful woman who is a leader and in full command of her energy and faculties. The archetype that is called for is more active than the Crone, more involved with the world, more in keeping with the energy of a mature and fully realized woman who is not yet ready to move into the Crone's introverted, introspective life.

The emerging archetype also reflects what we are seeing in our lives as women, we who are at the peak of our powers and abilities, and are not losing vitality like the waning moon, a symbol that has been identified with the Crone. We are at our lunar apex, our fullest potential, and able to make important and necessary contributions to our families and the world from a higher level of function and vision than ever before.

This ancient, yet new, archetype is the Queen.

Before we go further, let's define some terms. What is an *archetype?* In layman's terms, it is the primal form of an object or quality, the primal role model. One of the definitions Wikipedia lists is, "A statement, or pattern of behavior, a prototype upon which others are copied, patterned, or emulated."

The fourth-century philosopher, Plato, was the first to write about the idea of archetypes. He called them *forms,* and defined them as eternal descriptions of abstract concepts, such as Truth (with a capital T), which remain by essence unchanging despite endless manifestations.

For our purposes, the female archetypes shall be written as Maiden, Mother, Queen, and Crone with initial upper-case letters. For better or for worse, these archetypes carry with them all the emotional energy that the human psyche has invested in these ideas and have been handed down to us to wrestle with and measure ourselves against. Archetypes are much larger than our personal experiences of the qualities they carry. Think of them as universal concepts that appear in all cultures and carry the accumulated energy of all human experience. As such, they greatly influence human behavior and patterns.

Archetypes, as defined by the Swiss psychiatrist Carl Jung, one of the fathers of depth psychology, are "mythological associations, the motifs and images that can spring up anew anytime anywhere, independently of historical tradition or migration." Jung viewed mythic structures as reflective of the whole of the psyche and suggested: "It is possible to describe this [unconscious] content in rational, scientific language, but in this way one entirely fails to express its living character."

The traditional feminine trinity mentioned earlier, made up of Maiden, Mother, and Crone, symbolizes three phases of women's lives related to reproduction—essentially a virgin, a sexually active woman, and a menopausal woman (perhaps one who is less driven by her hormones to couple). Even though it has come to be considered a traditional depiction of the fertility cycle, it may be a relatively new concept. It originated or was popularized in the writing of a male mythologist, Robert Graves, after which it was adopted by present-day Wiccans and Neo-pagans who have found it meaningful and relevant to their lives.

Whether this iconography is ancient, or a modern tradition, is not what is being discussed here. In this book, I am simply using the three-stage concept as the starting point for considering the developmental stages of women's lives. What I am attempting to do is to make a case for the presence of—and our need as individuals for—a fourth developmental stage. Our longer productive stage of life calls for a more appropriate archetype: the Queen.

Archetypes and Greek Mythology

The ancient Greeks used the myths of their gods and goddesses as vehicles to express their understanding of human behavioral patterns. Besides believing in the divinity of these figures, just as other cultures believe in their own gods and goddesses, they also projected on to them their awareness of the archetypal patterns that play out in human life. It was through mythology that the ancient Greeks devised and developed psychological awareness.

In this book, we will look at various female archetypes through the familiar lenses of ancient Greek mythology. Of course, we could do something similar by exploring goddesses from other cultures, such as the goddesses of the Hindu pantheon from India, or of Native North, Central, and South America, but the Greek stories are the ones with which we are most likely to be familiar because of the educational model in our schools, which was handed down to us from European settlers. We can also look at our popular culture for other examples of these.

The Maiden

The Maiden archetype, often alternately called the Virgin, refers to the developmental phase of a woman's life that extends from her first menstrual period to motherhood. During this time of our lives as girls and then young women, we are not defined by our relationships with others. We are fully involved in our relationship with ourselves. The terms *maiden* and *virgin,* in this case, do not denote a lack of sexual experience, but instead indicate that she is "one unto herself." Historically, this is the period of life in which a young person is not defined by her connections to a man or to children, but only to the burgeoning possibilities of her life.

The world has changed a lot, hasn't it? It is understood by all contemporary Americans that a woman may be attracted to other women instead of men. And that some women will remain single their whole lives by choice or accident. Also, that women can lead fulfilling lives without centering them on raising children. But none of the societal progress that presents women with a greater range of options alters the fact that a young woman—like all young persons, male or female—is psychologically engaged in the problems of self-definition. She must determine her place in the world when she leaves the home of her parents or caregivers. How will she stand on her feet? What is her purpose in life?

Think back. When we were teenagers, the Maiden in each of us was unfolding and exploring who she was becoming. As Maidens, we were trying on different ways of presenting ourselves to ourselves and the world. As Maidens, we were subject to quick changes, just like the weather of spring, the season with which the Maiden archetype is associated. Spring is sunny one moment and pouring with rain the next. As were we emotionally. At that stage, our defining characteristics were possibilities and choices. We were in the process of becoming and had less baggage than later in life. The Maiden stage is associated with the waxing crescent moon, with its growing presence in the night sky and its promise of greater light to come.

The Greek goddesses who best represent the Maiden archetype are Artemis, Persephone before she is taken into the underworld by Hades, and Athena. Let's look at each of these three deities in turn.

Artemis. Artemis was known as the goddess of the forests and the wild animals that lived in them. As a virgin, she was complete in herself and did not need a man. She was the goddess of the wilds, practical, athletic, and adventurous. She liked physical culture, solitude, and was concerned with the protection of the environment. She protected animals and the young of all species, including young humans, as well as women in childbirth. Other areas under her protection were alternative lifestyles and women's communities. She was the quintessential tomboy.

Some of the frequently seen behavioral patterns for girls here: the love of animals and wanting to be involved in their care; the love of Nature; involvement in sports; and often a need for personal solitude.

Persephone, as the Kore. The story of Persephone and her mother, Demeter, is one of the best known of the Greek myths and illustrates the interaction between the feminine archetypes of Mother and Maiden. If you are a student of mythology, you may want to skip this retelling, but if you are like most of us, you may have only a fuzzy memory about this myth and the following will hopefully refresh your memory or introduce the age-old story.

As a Maiden, Persephone did not yet have a name, so she was referred to as the *Kore,* which means "the Girl." During this innocent stage of her life, she was in a meadow with her mother, the goddess Demeter, picking flowers, and was as unsullied and unaware as the flowers she gathered. In fact, she was the picture of innocent delight. Being that her mother was the goddess of the plant world, picking flowers was within her mother's province. As she is delighting in the joys of the spring of the year and of her life, the god of the underworld, Hades, bursts through the earth at her feet in his darkly glamorous chariot pulled by sleek black horses, and abducts the unsuspecting Kore, taking her with him to his underground kingdom.

If we were to rewrite this story in modern form, we might see a beautiful, unsuspecting young girl immersed in girlish pursuits, still in the care of her mother, being "taken" by a dark seducer into the underground of life. The abduction of the Kore demonstrates how unprepared those in the Maiden stage of life often are, and how unable they are to take precautions and exercise good judgment.

The rest of this story about how Demeter deals with the loss of her precious child will be described in the section on the Mother archetype.

Athena. There is an interesting story of the goddess Athena's birth that gives us direct insight into her primary characteristics. Zeus, her father, who continuously cheated on his wife, Hera, had seduced Metis, a divine being whose name means *knowledge.* When he found that Metis was pregnant, he feared she would have a son who would depose him, so he swallowed her whole. The unborn child continued to grow within Zeus and when he complained of horrible headaches, he had his skull opened to relieve the pain. Out sprang Athena fully clothed in armor and carrying a sword.

Since her mother, Metis, had been wholly subsumed into the energy of the masculine archetype as personified by her father, Zeus, she was deprived of even the slightest connection with her mother's and her own feminine body. And since she had little relationship with anything representing the feminine archetype, her myth follows a traditionally masculine path. Athena excels as a warrior and is an intellectual, a scholar, and politician.

This myth sheds light on why Athena is the goddess so strongly associated with "the father's daughter." Girls who are strongly connected with this archetype often find their identities and self-esteem in intellectual pursuits.

The Maiden Archetype in Popular Culture

If we were to look in our present-day popular culture for examples of the Maiden archetype, we might look at the TV sitcom personality of Sue Heck, the teenage daughter on *The Middle*. Sue is socially awkward and uncool, but upbeat and enthusiastic to the point of mania, and she seemingly never gives up. She is totally self-involved in the way teenagers often are, seeing everything only as it relates to her.

Adolescent narcissism is normal, not pathological, as it might be in an adult. The demands of growing up require a nearly complete immersion in the self to form the personality of the adult-to-be. Sue's character portrays this well, being aware of what others may be experiencing, but only as it relates to her.

Another, very different, and even more popular cultural example of the Maiden is real-life singer Miley Cyrus, particularly the persona she displayed as she performed at the 2013 Video Music Award ceremony. She caused a lot of controversy with her erotic singing and dancing. How she shook her derriere brought the word *twerking* into common usage, and her nearly ever-present extended tongue set other tongues wagging. The Maiden often delights in shocking others and showing her seductive side, delighting in the sexual power she intuitively knows is hers to use. And Cyrus portrayed the sexually experimenting aspect of the Maiden so well.

The Mother

The archetype of the Mother does not need much defining for most of us—only a broadening of the scope it embraces. It goes without saying that all the attributes a woman must have and cultivate to bring to birth and then adulthood a viable human being are part of this archetype's realm. But this archetypal energy may also be used to successfully gestate, birth, and raise a career, a business, creative works, a spiritual path, or any other endeavor a woman may wish to pursue temporarily or make her ongoing life's work. So, as a positive, developmental archetype, we may include all women in the Mother's domain.

Under the Mother archetype, the early period of our adult lives—let's say generally from the mid-twenties to the mid-forties—will bring forth the qualities we associate with motherhood: a commitment to the care and protection of children or creations, and the devotion and unwavering sense of responsibility needed to raise these "children" to their own full, independent adulthood.

The positive Mother archetype infuses women with the ability to move their own needs, wants, and desires into second place, and replace them with doing and being whatever is necessary for the sake of their children. A woman moving from the "one unto herself" of the Maiden may be amazed at how much and how often she now willingly puts her own interests aside when it comes to her baby.

This is hands-on, personal mothering—a day and night job—where the woman's focus is survival, growth, and protection of her offspring and every decision she makes will prioritize them before anyone else, including herself.

The Mother Archetype in Greek Mythology

In Greek mythology, the goddess Demeter, whom we met briefly when discussing the Maiden in the form of the Kore (see page 7) epitomizes the positive archetype of the devoted mother. When her daughter was abducted and taken to the underworld by Hades, Demeter was shredded by grief. She looked everywhere for her lost daughter, neglecting her duties as the goddess of the crops. Because of her distraction in looking for her daughter and her increasing grief and depression, however, she allowed the crops to die in the fields before they could be harvested. People starved and implored Demeter to return to her duties, but as a bereft mother, she could not.

The myth continues with Demeter finding out what happened to her daughter: Zeus, the king of the Gods, had allowed Hades to take her daughter to be his wife. Learning this, Demeter demands that Zeus make Hades give up Persephone and return her. Finally, Zeus agrees, mainly because everybody is starving, but then it is discovered that Persephone (no longer "the girl," but now a woman with her own name) has eaten a few pomegranate seeds while in the underworld—meaning she will forever be tied to Hades and the place where he lives. In ancient Greece, the pomegranate was viewed as a symbol of fertility owing to its innumerable seeds. The implication is that Persephone and Hades have made love and are bonded. A compromise is reached whereby Persephone can return to her mother for nine months of the year, but she must return to the underworld for the other three—the months of winter.

Demeter's sense of loss continues to be felt by everybody else during the cold months when nothing grows. But the sun shines brightly and there is abundant growth when Demeter has her daughter back every spring.

This story of Demeter's unwavering search and reunion with her daughter gives a strong testament to power of a mother's love.

The premier example of the Mother archetype in the Christian tradition, which supplanted the ancient Greek tradition, is Mary, the mother of Jesus. Her devotion to her son and the worthiness she portrayed to be equal to the challenge of being the mother of God makes her an embodiment of the positive Mother archetype.

The Mother Archetype in Popular Culture

There are so many depictions of the devoted Mother archetype in popular culture that it is nearly impossible to single one out. For the sake of an example of a Mother, let's look at the movie *Mildred Pierce,* whose lead character is a woman who attempts to please her child to both their detriment. The original film starred Joan Crawford and was later remade for television as a mini-series starring Kate Winslet. Here's how the story goes.

Mildred Pierce has worked hard to provide for her two daughters during the Great Depression. Set in Southern California in 1931, she is a hardworking, recently divorced mother, who has no employable skills, but since she is an excellent baker, she decides to make and sell pies. Over the years, she builds her pie shop into three successful restaurants. Her younger daughter dies from pneumonia and Mildred buries her grief in her work. She is determined to give her remaining daughter, Veda, everything she wants and all that she herself did not have. She is devastated when she realizes her daughter is embarrassed by her humble beginnings as waitress and a baker but continues to try and win her daughter's approval by supporting Veda and attempting to raise her social standing by entering a loveless marriage with a playboy, Monte.

Spoiler alert. The twist is that Monte runs through Mildred's money and when she goes to confront him, finds her daughter, Veda, in his arms. Whereupon, Monte tells Mildred he would never marry a tramp like Veda, and Veda shoots and kills him. Veda tries yet again to enlist her mother's help by proclaiming her love and regret for all she has done. Mildred refuses to help her and calls the police. The next scene shows them both in the interrogation room where Veda is being charged with the murder.

True to the pattern inherent in the archetype of the self-sacrificing Mother, Mildred takes responsibility for everything. She tells Veda, "I am sorry. I tried."

Today, nobody would claim that Mildred Pierce is a psychologically healthy woman. But her story is perhaps best seen as illustrative of the limited choices faced by a woman of her time. Original audiences may or may not have viewed her behavior as appropriate, but they would have understood it—though it certainly led to a tragic outcome. Not only does the script reveal the awful paradigm of needing to be married to be considered "good enough," it depicts the awful consequences of classism. As a morality tale, it pits the corrupt and overly self-interested Maiden against the moral and overly self-effacing Mother.

Some other depictions of women under the archetypal energy of the ridiculously "good" Mother would include many women from early TV sitcoms: Donna Reed, Harriet Nelson, and June Cleaver. These depictions portrayed the mothers as one-dimensional, usually having no life or interests of their own and being satisfied just to be moms and wives.

Real-life women, of course, are multifaceted. Even though we are decades beyond those fictional women, their stereotypes continue to haunt us from the regions of our subconscious minds and the collective unconscious.

The Shadow Side of the Mother

Carl Jung used the term *shadow* to describe the unwanted, rejected aspects of an individual's psyche that are relegated to the realm of the unconscious, where they are acted out with little or no awareness. The shadow aspects of our personalities and our desires are not necessarily negative, although we may feel that way about them.

Sometimes shadow issues are those that do not adhere to the social mores of the era in which we live. We find the dissonance between how we secretly wish to be and how we feel that we must be to fit in with the people around us painful, so we reject the part of us that is causing the friction. A psychologically healthy person ultimately learns to embrace the shadow; otherwise she finds it projected outwardly through her choices, which may be self-defeating.

All archetypes have shadow aspects. The shadow aspects of the Mother archetype include images of the abandoning mother, the devouring (smothering) mother, the absent mother, and the all-powerful mother. Today, there are new variations on the theme of the absent mother, which may include the addict mother and the working mother.

Please note that I am not intentionally casting aspersions on working mothers, only acknowledging that they are sometimes perceived in our culture as a variation, for obvious reasons, of the absent mother. A working mother's shadow may be the secret of her preference for her career over her kids. A stay-at-home mother's shadow may be her desire to live through her children and claim their accomplishments as her own—not letting them separate.

Accusing a woman of putting her self-interests on a par with those of her children is used as a means with which to berate and shame contemporary women. But if you study all the possible variations of the Mother archetype, you can find plenty of ways to shame stay-at-home women, too. It might be better simply to let other women lead their lives and not try to shame them or ourselves at all!

The Crone

In the paradigm of the Triple Goddess, the Crone is seen as the third and final archetype in women's lives. It is at the core of this book's mission, however, to show the Crone as the fourth life stage, coming after the Queen. At her essence, the Queen is a blending of the Mother and the Crone.

The following is the traditional depiction of the Crone archetype.

The Crone is a teacher, a mature woman who carries the perspective of the community in addition to her personal perspective.

An elder, she cares about the well-being of the community and its culture. She sees things clearly, is of a spiritual nature, and has an internal beauty. The Crone is wise, powerful, and holy woman.

The Crone is a woman who has developed a sense of her own empowerment through her relational nature. She has become a teacher or guide watching over the lives of individuals and the fabric of the whole community or family. She is keenly aware of all that surrounds her, while also being deeply in touch with her own subjective perceptions, and she is able to share her views and values for the benefit of all. While taking seriously her role of caring for the whole, she has a playful spirit and approaches life in a lighthearted way. It may surprise you to think of a Crone as having a light-hearted aspect, but the Greek goddess Baubo illustrates that quality beautifully. When Demeter (remember her?) was wandering the earth in mourning for her lost daughter. Demeter came to rest in the city of Eleusis, where she took momentary respite in the house of the king. She became the nanny of the king's son. Many of the household servants saw that this was a very sad and depressed woman and did their best to bring her out of her gloom. One of the servants was the disguised goddess Baubo, described as an old woman. Baubo tried to amuse Demeter to help disrupt her mourning. She made off-color remarks and noticed these brought a bit of a smile to Demeter's face. She continued in this way to amuse, allowing her remarks to become even more risqué and then with great flare she lifted her skirts completely, showing her vulva. Demeter responded with a hearty belly laugh at this surprising display which helped her dispel her mourning. Somewhat restored, Demeter's depression turned to righteous anger and she demanded Zeus to order Hades to release her daughter.

Baubo shows us the power of hilarity to overcome low spirits and how this quality is often an attribute of the Crone.

Having the ability to sense the whole of things requires balance, internal and external. This last phase of life is a time of integration and acceptance, a time for emergence of a woman secure in herself and at peace with her being.

A Crone develops an outward expression of her spirituality and awareness. She is aware of a connection to the earth and to her self-defined spirituality it as well, which is expressed in ritual both personal and communal.

In *Goddesses in Older Women*, psychiatrist and Jungian analyst Jean

Shinoda Bolen, M.D., describes this stage of a woman's development also as a time when "thoughts turn to death and divinity, or mortality and eternity, or our religious beliefs and personal faith." This phase "is when the subject of death invites us to think about the meaning of life."

Centuries ago, there was a belief that a woman became a Crone at menopause, when her blood ceased to flow regularly. It was believed that post-menopausal women and pregnant women held their blood inside their bodies, but rather than producing a baby, this "keeping in" for older women promoted their becoming sages. The Crone was often seen as a healer, who tended the sick and dying because she knew the use of herbal and other natural medicines.

As actress and playwright Donna Wilshire notes in her book *Virgin, Mother, Crone*:

> Crones were the ones most capable of offering guidance and direction to others, the most likely persons to have the wisdom, the time and experience to heal the sick and minister to the dying. But time factoring was their special responsibility.
>
> Menstruating women's bodies kept track of—were—lunar-month calendars while the old, remembering women kept track of—embodied—long-range events. It was their ability to respond to large cycles that kept all events in perspective.

In the contemporary world, cronehood is a time of accepting the body's limitations with compassion, keeping mentally active, encouraging those younger than us, surrendering the ego, and also of receiving help and consideration from others. Shadow issues of women at the end of life may involve dealing with melancholy or depression and absorption in the aging process. Goddess archetypes that may represent this stage of life are Sophia and Hecate.

Hecate. Hecate was the Greek name for an ancient pre-Olympian, underground goddess. In a poem by Hesiod, *Theogony,* he writes of her inclusion by Zeus into the community of Olympian deities. This incorporation of her into the Greek pantheon brought her respect and gave her relevance to eighth-century B.C.E. Greeks.

...Hecate, whom Zeus, the son of Cronos, honored above all. He gave her splendid gifts, to have a share of the earth and the unplowed sea. She received honor also in starry heaven, and is honored exceedingly by the deathless gods. For to this day, whenever any one of men on earth offers rich sacrifices and prays for favor according to custom, he calls upon Hecate. Great honor comes fully easily to him whose prayers the goddess receives favorably, and she bestows wealth upon him; for the power surely is with her. For as many as were born of Earth and Ocean amongst all these she has her due portion. The son of Cronos did her no wrong nor took anything away of all that was her portion among the former Titan gods; but she holds as the division was at the first from the beginning, privilege both in earth, and in heaven, and in sea.

We can see from the foregoing passage that Hecate was highly revered by the ancients, both publicly and as a household goddess, who reflected an awareness of the unending cycle of birth, death, and rebirth for her worshippers.

The Crone archetype's province is death and rebirth. Inherent in the paradigm of nature is decay and degeneration of all living things, breaking them down into their component parts and simplest elements so as to recycle them. Of all the Crone's areas of dominion this is the hardest for contemporary Westerners to contemplate, much less appreciate. As an industrialized, mainly urban population, we have lost connection with the cycle of life, death, and rebirth. Farmers and gardeners, who are involved with the unending repetition of Nature's seasons are keenly aware of the importance of death and decay, while the rest of us do not wish to be witness to it. Much of the fear of the Crone has its roots in this reminder of the final ending and decay of all that lives. She embodies, for many people, their own fear of death.

Because of the goddess Hecate's connection with life's end, her skill at healing the sick with the use of herbs and other remedies are emblematic of the Crone. Other attributes of the Crone include midwifery and tending the dying. Crones were women who would call on their long experience to keep alive the oral traditions of their families and cultures; knowledge of these enabled them to counsel others and provided the community with the ability to foresee outcomes by studying patterns in the past.

The word *Crone* is an archaic form of the word *crown,* and so we know that originally it was an honorable term. Over the millennia, it has been denigrated to mean an ugly old woman, who is somewhat witchlike in her appearance, and perhaps is more comical than wise, but certainly scarier than any witch. She is shown either as possessing unknown powers or as a powerless, feeble figure.

Between the Mother and the Crone

As we can see from studying the Mother and the Crone, there are several areas in which these archetypes overlap. Psychologically, this is true of all developmental stages: One stage does not end abruptly as we move on to the next. We retain the skills we've accumulated. All development is gradual, with the Mother eventually transitioning to the Crone. But it seems like an overly long stretch for a woman developmentally to move from birthing and raising children (or her own creations) to thirty years later overseeing and participating in the eventuality of death, decay and rebirth. This begs the question, what exactly is happening with women during our midlives, a period of decades in which we remain active and contributing members of our society? It would seem that during this time of life it would be appropriate for us to move away from the active role of a mother and toward a higher place where we can view events and people with increased perspective.

Put another way, active mothering is hands-on, in-the-trenches kind of work. (Remember, mothering is not only biological, it may be seen to extend to all that a woman gives birth to.) In a corporate sense, the Mother would be a mid-management position. In the army, she would be a sergeant. By contrast, the Queen archetype, coming between the Mother and the Crone, has more status and authority. The Queen is an executive. She is like a general in the military.

The Queen combines the recent experience of the day-to-day work (the Mother) with the Crone's higher, broader vision of life experience.

Other Archetypal Systems

I feel that at this point it is important to look at some of the other feminine archetypal systems people have developed. Primary among these is the one established by Toni Wolff.

Psychologist Toni Wolff, former president of the Psychologischer Club Zürich after being the first woman elected to its executive board, was a protégé of C.G. Jung, editor of his collected papers, and an instructor of analyst candidates the C.G. Jung Institute from its founding in 1948, described four (notice *four*) feminine archetypes in her writing: the Mother, the Hetaira, the Medial Woman, and the Amazon. Her designations were more along the lines of lifelong personality types than, as I am suggesting, progressive developmental stages. But before examining in greater detail how her system works, it is necessary to explain the terms she uses since some of them are not in general use.

Wolff's Mother. Wolff gives the term *Mother* roughly the same meaning as I do, using it to signify a woman's natural and sacred ability to conceive, give birth, then sustain and renew life by her maternal abilities to cherish, nurse, help, and teach. How might this archetype show up in a woman's life?

Susan fully embraced the Mother Archetype. Married for twelve years, her primary focus was on her four children. She identified her role of caring and looking after their many needs and wants as the center of her existence and drew much of her personal identity from being a mother. She had a satisfactory relationship with her husband, but she often felt she lumped his needs into the same hopper as those of her children. If truth be told, Susan saw her husband as another of her children.

The Hetaira. The term *Hetaira* originally referred to a highly cultured courtesan or concubine, especially in ancient Greece. In a more modern sense, it can mean a friend, companion, or mistress. She is any woman whose primary connection is with a man. The Hetaira also embodies the Lover archetype. This woman is not primarily interested in family or community. Instead she is focused on a one-on-one relationship with an individual man wherein she may challenge him to excel and in return to be challenged by him. Perhaps Toni Wolff recognized this archetype because she was Carl

Jung's lover as well as his student. She lived in an era in which accomplished professional women were rarely given their due; some of their status came from being linked to significant colleagues.

How might this archetype show up in a woman's life? June is a good example of a Hetaira. Although the mother of two children, she always saw her primary relationship as being with her husband. She did not ignore or neglect her children, but her heart and her focus were always with her husband and their relationship. She had taken time early on in their marriage to get to know him intimately: his likes and dislikes, his goals and dreams. Now in midlife, she also works on her physical and mental attributes to continue to attract and reengage him. She defines herself as a companion, lover, and wife.

As we can see, each of these two designations position the archetypal energy within the relationship to another person: The Mother's primary relationship is with her child, the Hetaira's relationship is with an individual man. The next two archetypes connect differently.

The Medial Woman. A woman embodying the Medial Woman archetype is focused on the unknown, whether that means she makes attempts to predict cultural trends or functions as a seer. She is often attracted to a spiritual path, or she may find the field of psychology of compelling interest. She relies on intuition more heavily than information from her five senses to find her truths. In other words, rather than through what she sees or hears, she gets her information from the outside world through a sometimes vague, innate knowing. Her skill is in easily picking up on patterns, rather than items. She sees the whole forest and is less likely to focus on one tree.

How might this archetype show up in a woman's life? Sylvia has always had a vivid imagination and now as an adult has found her talent for knowing the next step in any situation to be a great gift. She works as a successful strategist for a large public relations firm, using her uncanny "knowing" to predict trends in the international marketplace. Her Medial Woman qualities help her see which trends are evolving strongly and in which direction public opinion is moving.

The Amazon. Amazons are women whose primary focus is with competition or challenge. The Amazon connects with others almost exclusively on an impersonal basis, unlike the Mother and Hetaira.

She is the female version of the masculine Warrior archetype. As such, she is dedicated in an impersonal way to whatever battles or challenges have engaged her. In other words, her connection is to her cause rather than to a person. The Amazon archetype can overlap with the Mother archetype when we consider what a mother might do to keep her children safe. But the Amazon is not primarily driven or inspired to nurture her own children. The Amazon is often a physically oriented woman, one who prefers action to thought. She is willing to fight for a cause she believes in and holds her ground.

How might this archetype show up in a woman's life? Casey has lived her life as an Amazon. As a teen, she realized she had strong feelings about helping those who were not adequately able to help themselves. At first her attention was drawn to the plight of unwanted, often abused animals. She collected strays in her neighborhood, cleaned them up, nursed them, and did all she could to find them homes. Later, when she was older, she became an activist for Greenpeace, raising money to fund their many attempts to block the slaughter of baby seals. Her bravery is exemplary. She has had personal confrontations with angry seal hunters, who saw her as getting in the way of their making a living.

Toni Wolff saw these four feminine archetypes as being positioned in a four-sided arrangement, with each archetype placed across from an "opposite" and being flanked by two others to which she could relate. For instance, the two person-connected archetypes, the Mother and Hetaira, stand across from each other. The Amazon and the Medial Woman archetypes, to which they can both relate, flank them. This means that the Mother can incorporate qualities of the Amazon when it is necessary to champion or protect her children. Likewise, the Amazon is often prompted in her work by maternal feelings, as we saw with Casey and the stray animals she rescued.

The Hetaira, in her quest to challenge her man as well as herself, may take on difficult tasks, such as learning and succeeding in areas of interest to her man. Both the Mother and the Hetaira may access qualities of the Medial woman, such as her spirituality or psychology, to further their success in the primary archetypal roles.

What I find most compelling in Toni Wolff's archetypal system is her conclusion. Note that the bold emphasis below is mine.

When all four axes (Mother, Hetaira, Amazon, and Medial Woman) are finally made conscious and integrated into a woman's personal psyche, the archetype of the Queen is constellated which embodies all of the attributes of each axis in consciousness. **This can only be done with difficulty and during the latter part of life.**

I see this passage as supporting my case for the Queen being a *developmental* archetype, which shows up when we have brought together all the qualities of our disparate experiences and integrated them into one woman's soul. Having achieved a level of wholeness is that which allows her to gain the elevated perspective of the Queen. I believe it is this elevated perspective that gives the Queen her power.

Since the basic premise of this book is the addition of a *fourth* developmental archetype (Maid, Mother, Queen, and Crone) into the already existing grouping of three archetypes, I think it is interesting to look a little deeper into the qualities attributed to the number four. Things tend to be grouped in fours: there are four seasons, four directions, four elements, and four phases of the moon. Carl Jung postulated four types of cognitive function: thinking, feeling, sensing, and intuiting. You may have run across these designations if an employer ever gave you a Myers-Briggs personality assessment. Four is stable: four-legged chairs are much less likely to tip than three-legged chairs.

According to an article by Robert L. Johnson, Ph.D., published in the newsletter *Jungian Life,* "The formation of quaternities in Jungian thinking is quite common. Jung thought that *all complete systems were four-fold.*" Because of the stability of the number four, there is something about the number four that speaks to wholeness, and a sense of completion.

When a triad becomes a quaternity, everything seems to fit on an intuitive level and it all seems to move up more than a notch.

Another interesting theory on feminine archetypes that I discovered in my research is one postulated by midwives Elizabeth Davis and Carol Leonard in their book *The Women's Wheel of Life.* They identify thirteen feminine archetypes: Daughter, Maiden, Blood Sister, Lover, Mother, Midwife, Amazon, Matriarch, Priestess, Sorceress, Crone, Dark Mother, and in the center of the wheel is the Transformer. Each stage in their system is finely detailed since there are thirteen named types, rather than four; and many, in my opinion, of these types are overlapping. As former midwives, there is a strongly felt influence of the psychology of the blood mysteries (menarche, childbirth, and menopause) in their work. The number thirteen correlates with the number of lunar cycles in any given year. And the moon is considered feminine since it reflects the masculine light of the sun.

Any woman drawn to explore the depth psychology perspective may find their work illuminating—no pun intended.

Of course, it goes without saying, the traditional Maid, Mother, and Crone trinity is interwoven with their approach.

CHAPTER 2

WOMEN AND POWER

Of the other archetypes in this quaternity of Maid, Mother, Queen, and Crone, as stated in the last chapter, I believe the Queen is the most connected to worldly power. She has a lifetime of experience, and now has the tools to use to implement her vision, and from her elevated perspective is wise in the way of the world. She is intimately knowledgeable about power—who has power, and how is it being held and used—so it seems appropriate to examine the history of women's power. What are the ways we regard power? How have society's views of women shaped our lives? How have our cultural beliefs fostered or interfered with our claims to our own personal power?

Women's relationship with power has been a difficult one. On a purely physical level there are some obvious inequalities—one of which is that men have more upper body strength and longer legs, making it easy for them to overpower women after they go through puberty. The other, perhaps most important element is that women usually need the help and protection of men at some point in their lives, most commonly when they are pregnant or nursing.

At present what has been called the patriarchy is the pattern for and repository of power for most of the cultures of the world. Women have not been accorded a place of power within this construct to hold or exercise personal power. It is only with rare exception that an individual woman has been allowed to hold and use her power. An example might be Elizabeth I of England, who, because she was the lawful and acknowledged Queen of England, wielded power as its Queen, but that power was not hers to pass onto another woman, but to have it revert to the laws governing succession to the throne. To see how the patriarchy continues to impact women's access to power, we will take a look at some of the reasons it continues to keep women's power at a low and, for them, manageable level.

A Brief History of the Patriarchy

The patriarchy is a worldwide culture of domination, maintained by both men and women. I would like to conjecture how it may have begun, and how it spread to become a major tenet of the law and culture, even the very fabric of life in most parts of the world, and how it continues to limit the power of women at all stages of life. Even with the rise of feminism in the nineteenth and twentieth centuries, to the present day, the patriarchy is still woven, although somewhat less visibly, into our lives.

Patriarchy is a system that promotes male privilege by being male dominated, male identified, and male centered. It is also organized around an obsession with control and involves, as just one of its aspects, the oppression and control of women.

The real truth is that as a domination model patriarchy oppresses some men, children, and nature as well. It is built on the concept that there is a privileged station in life. Those who would occupy this station can only do so at the expense of all others who would lay claim to it. Patriarchy sets itself up to value only those who are part of this ruling class, in this case, men. But not all men. Only the "right men." Right Men may be defined as being this or that, or the other thing. There are any number of exclusions that may exist, but the first default setting is being male. Other qualities that admit or exclude men to the elite are race, money, family, accomplishment, age, religion, social standing, sexual orientation, and more. Because women don't possess the requisite gender, we shouldn't even think of applying.

Has patriarchy always been the underlying structure, and if not, what else existed in its place? How did it begin and how did it get to be nearly universal? These are some questions that come to mind. Mainstream history doesn't address these questions, but when it is reported in our textbooks, history gives the impression that everything has always been this way. One of the few views I have found that differ from the assumption that the patriarchy always existed is articulated by cultural historian and systems scientist, Riane Eisler, in The *Chalice and the Blade*. Her book introduces the concepts of dominator and partnership cultures. Reading her work helped me begin to look at the feminine archetypes through the lens of power.

Archaeologist Marija Gimbutas, a specialist in Neolithic and Bronze Age cultures in the region of Europe, offers a complementary view in her seminal work, *The Gods and Goddesses of Ancient Europe*. In her book, Gimbutas proposes that a partnership culture was prominent in prehistoric Europe, lasting on up to the era of the Minoan culture in the Mediterranean (circa 2,500 B.C.E.). In this culture, a Great Mother goddess—let's call her the Goddess—was worshipped and mortal women were revered as life-givers. Women were even often seen as having magical powers.

Eisler takes the possibility further. She asserts that a culture of peace and reverence for life existed for many centuries that emphasized love and respect for nature. In this culture which she postulates existed in our prehistory, men and women worked as partners with both making equally valued contributions to society.

Eisler also posits that approximately 1,500 years before the advent of Christianity, the Goddess-centered life of the partnership society was overrun and supplanted by a male-dominated, warrior society through an invasion that may have come from Western Asia and India. The Goddess worshipers were defeated, and the Goddess was made to take a lesser position in relation to the gods of the warrior society.

Goddess worship did not disappear completely but continued to exist in pockets of Europe and the Mediterranean for some time. By the time of classical Greece and the rise of the Roman Empire, male-dominated society was firmly in place, supported by its masculine deities. Patriarchy was the order of the day.

Perhaps Eisler's most important contribution to contemporary women is to make the case that domination of women by men is not necessarily the only template for human society. Whether the ancient partnership model successfully existed or not, the idea is worthy of our attention because we are moving toward a successful partnership culture in our own society at present. It is a big step, causing us to change our sense of possibility at every stage of our lives as women.

Before we go there, let's first look at how many scholars believe the patriarchal system evolved. When growing foods and tending animals (agriculture) replaced hunting and gathering as a means of survival for our prehistoric ancestors, human civilization was born. Staying in one place, rather than leading a nomadic life, allowed ongoing, cohesive communities to be established. Whether this agricultural life was female-centered, peaceful, and Goddess-worshiping, as envisioned by Gimbutas and Eisler, is still open to debate. But what is clear is that whether through an invasion of warrior-led, male deity-worshiping hordes who overthrew the matriarchy or through a more gradual shift of power, by 1,500 B.C.E. agricultural civilization was patriarchal. Men ran the political, social, and cultural life of the community.

As agricultural societies grew and prospered, becoming more complex, women's power positions within them declined. Agricultural society was based on ownership and the primary ownership was of the land. For the most part, men owned the land. But if a woman owned property (in many societies, that was not allowed), then the woman's land usually passed to her husband when she married. Arranged marriages ensured that the wife's property was what made her desirable as a wife. That property was her dowry and it afforded her some marital leverage, but society was not a level playing field for men and women.

It was also usual that the wife would move into the orbit of her husband's family at marriage, where she had little personal or social support. So, with her property no longer under her control and no easy connection to her family of origin, a wife was easily relegated to a "one down" position.

Women's positions in society and within the family differed in many ancient cultures. Early Sumerians (circa 5,500–4000 B.C.E.) may have given women more power than they did later. Their religion attributed considerable power to female sexuality and women were accorded rights under the law so that they couldn't be considered property outright, but the archeological record shows that the law was not equitable in many ways. For instance, the punishment for marital infidelity was far harsher for women than men.

Mesopotamian society succeeded the Sumerian era with its emphasis on the woman's virginity upon marriage and dictated that respectable women wear veils in public as a symbol of their modesty. Eventually women's social positions and their abilities to participate fully in the life of the community eroded more completely. Finally, the law began to dictate more of what women could do and could not do, until a good part of Mesopotamian law was mostly comprised of limitations and restrictions for women, as well as assuring some basic protections to them.

Egypt was somewhat of an exception in antiquity. It gave upper-class women more leeway and Egypt produced some remarkably powerful queens, such as Hand Nefertiti.

Hatshepsut was the daughter of King Thutmose I. When he died, her half-brother, a son of Thutmose I, ascended to the throne and following tradition, married his father's oldest daughter. Thutmose II ruled for only a few years and died at an early age. Thutmose II had had a son by another queen, who succeeded him on the throne. Since the new pharaoh, Thutmose III, was very young, Hatshepsut became his regent and she ruled in his stead for six years. In 1473 B.C.E., Hatshepsut tired of ruling on behalf of the child and boldly proclaimed herself as pharaoh. To ensure her place on the throne, she needed two things: the support of the priests, and for herself to be seen as divine. She told a story which was widely spread that her mother had been visited while pregnant by the god Amon-Ra, which indicated her divinity and legitimized her claim. She also sought and gained the support of the priesthood, which further strengthened her claim. To appear even more pharaoh-like she dispensed with feminine clothing and wore only male pharaoh garb. This included wearing a fake beard like the ones worn by previous male rulers. Hatshepsut was a very successful ruler of Egypt: she established trade routes and oversaw numerous construction projects rather than engaging in war to increase the size of the lands under her control. She is considered, in fact, to have been one of the most accomplished leaders of Ancient Egypt.

Nefertiti was the chief wife of the pharaoh Akhenaton and at one point during his reign was believed to have co-ruled with him. She was often shown in hieroglyphics as conducting royal business on her own, without him present.

But two Egyptian queens do not equality make. Lest you think life in ancient Egypt was idyllic for average women, consider the words of Ptah Hotep, an Egyptian writer circa 2,000 B.C.E.

> If you are a man of note, find for yourself a household, and love your wife at home as it beseems. Fill her belly . . . clothe her back . . . but hold her back from getting the mastery. Remember that her eye is her storm wind, and her vulva and her mouth are her strength.

There, of course, were other women who rose to high places in particular times under particular circumstances, but it seems safe to say that by the time of the Roman Empire, with its network of roads and imperial connections linking the known world, which were able to carry not only goods and government, but also ideas, philosophies, and religions far and wide, that the patriarchy was well entrenched throughout the entire Western world.

The early Christian Church, still an underground movement, was part of this world and wealthy widows often hosted meetings of early disciples and their followers in their homes. They also often preached and officiated at these clandestine gatherings, but this seeming equality would not last. When Christianity was finally recognized and became the official religion of the Roman Empire through the conversion of Constantine in 312 C.E. it became more accepted and institutionalized, taking on the misogynistic ideas that pervaded Roman society. The Church began to systematically reduce the importance of women to conform to the prevailing attitudes.

Among other symbolic losses was the loss of Eve. Eve began to be seen as the cause of Adam's downfall and subsequently as the primary cause of Christ's death and humanity's need for salvation. Mary Magdalene was mistaken for a prostitute by a pope, who confused her with another biblical woman, and she then carried that designation until the discovery of the Dead Sea Scrolls in Nag Hammadi, Egypt, in 1945. The Church formally admitted its mistake finally in 1956, but many Catholics still believe she was a whore to this day even so.

Third-century Christians decided menstruation was unclean, and thereafter menstruating women could not approach the altar. Women had never been given the title of priestess by Christians, only that of deaconess. But even so, they could not fulfill their deacons' duties if they were bleeding. Because of this separation from men and the judging of them to be inferior, the treatment of women became harsher and crueler, until after centuries of denigration women were considered subhuman and a danger to men.

This antipathy culminated in the "Burning Times" of the late medieval era, when it is now believed that perhaps as many as 100,000 people (mostly women) were tortured and killed over the 400 years of the Inquisition.

Many historical elements converged to form this "perfect storm." The beginnings of a medical profession found the herbalist/midwife a threat to the stature of physicians as healers. The emerging law profession needed an arena in which to practice and seizing the property of those accused of witchcraft was highly lucrative. Combine this with the fact that women were now universally considered inferior and, if unattached and not under the protection of a man, they could be preyed upon with impunity, and you're in business. Also, the Church was feeling threatened by the unstoppable move towards reformation. Demonizing women and offering up a scapegoat was a way to bind their believers to the faith more closely.

Until very recently, women did not have the right to vote for their own representation in democracies, they could not get a bank loan or open a checking account in their own names and had to rely on their husband's sponsorship in the financial arena. Women are still fighting in the courts for their reproductive rights, equal pay, and opportunities in the Western nations. We've come a long way, but parity and partnership between the genders has not arrived yet.

Internalized Misogyny

As often happens, if one is subjected to nearly universal beliefs of one's unworthiness and inferiority for long enough, these beliefs will be taken in and given credence. So, it is with us women. Psychologists call this type of idea an *introject*. We are socialized as children, learning about the culture we live in through our many experiences. Attitudes, beliefs, and behaviors are observed and participated in at a young age and these become a part of our internal reality. This is generally done in a way of which we are not overly aware.

We operate on these unexamined ideas and ways of being until they are challenged. Then we might reaccept them as truth or "just the way things are," or we may examine them and, if found without merit, discard them.

As a woman, you may feel you are completely supportive of women's equality. You may have joined the first Women's March in 2017. You may even have participated in the Women's Movement of the 1970s and 1980s, a movement that brought broad and far-reaching changes to our culture. Or perhaps you remember that your mother and her friends participated. However, there are still serious and disturbing remnants of discrimination, and some of this seems to come from women ourselves. Usually thoughtful women, often unwittingly engage in girl bashing in the most unconscious ways. Often this comes in the form of praise for another woman, with a somewhat hidden disqualifier.

Play a little game with me. Take notice of every time you think or talk about another woman. Is it fully supportive or is there a little (or big) undercurrent of criticism in your remarks? If you are like me, you may find there is some less-than-supportive or unfair element in your thoughts or conversation.

Take this game one step further. Do these thoughts and remarks help or hurt us as women?

You may recognize that when you speak or think negatively of another woman you take some part of the positive energy away. For example, you may remark that you admire a woman in public life, such as former U.S. Attorney General Madeleine Albright, and then also comment on her age or lack of physical beauty. You might say how much you admire all that Oprah Winfrey has accomplished, but also say how she seems unable to ever get control of her weight problem.

Would you make such comments about men of comparable achievement? Of course not.

How about demeaning the accomplishments of other women by noting that they have failed (in your opinion) in some other traditionally feminine arena? Perhaps, you comment on the successful businesswoman whose children did not turn out so well.

To feel better about ourselves and our accomplishments, we need to take real pleasure in the success of other women and stop seeing it as a threat. Competition divides us, whereas support of one another will enhance us all. Queens do not stoop to trashing other queens. It is beneath them. A woman embodying the Queen archetype sets the standard by respecting others as she respects herself.

Since the first draft of this book was written, it has become clear that the changes in women's rights realized in the 1960s and 1970s have been largely inadequate and are now up for review and revitalization. Grassroots movements like #MeToo and #TimesUp have made their presences known and are heralding a resurgence of feminism.

The Partnership Model

So far, we have looked at the model of the dominator culture, which the patriarchy represents. But what might take its place and lessen the inequality between men and women? Surely, we don't want just to see the pendulum swing to the other extreme, resulting in a return to matriarchy. According to Riane Eisler, the partnership model has in the past, and would again allow, people of both genders to contribute more equally to one another and enable them to be seen (and see themselves) as indispensable to balance the quality of life for one another.

A basic difference between the dominator culture and the partnership culture is that domination is founded on a one-up, one-down relationship—a hierarchy—whereas partnership relies of the concept of "linking." In linking, elements are connected to one another, with give and take and mutual support being the underlying concepts.

It is not hard to see which of the two models promotes cooperation between respected participants—and which is more favorable to women. The dominator model promotes aggression, force, and subjugation. The partnership model reinforces mutual benefits, equality, cooperation, and peacefulness.

On the subject of partnership, Riane Eisler in *The Power of Partnership* (2002) says:

> In the Partnership model you find a democratic and egalitarian social structure, equal partnership between women and men, and less socially accepted violence in all relations—from intimate to international—because violence is not needed to maintain rigid rankings of domination. You also find beliefs about human nature that support empathic and mutually respectful relations. And you see qualities denigrated as "feminine" in the domination model, such as caring and non-violence, are valued in men and women, and guide social policy.

In *Gods and Goddesses of Old Europe*, Marija Gimbutas makes a convincing case for the existence of several millennia of a peaceful, Goddess-centered, village life with no evidence of war. There were no artifacts found of weapons, no skeletons with fatal injuries

31

inflicted by weapons, no fortified buildings or trenches. The artifacts which were found were the remnants of household goods, and 92 percent of the statues found between 30,000 and 3,000 B.C.E. were of women or goddesses, many of which were portrayed as pregnant or lactating.

From the foregoing, I would like to suggest that the partnership model has successfully existed in the past and could do so again in the future. Not only is it a viable possibility; it also may well be our only choice for survival since the increased technology fostered by a war-mongering dominator culture has given us the ability to destroy our own civilization as well as our planet.

In terms of the personal psychology of women at midlife, spending her life as a participant in the partnership model allows a woman to develop a sense of personal agency and power that being a dominated participant denies. We can only successfully operate and grow within our lives if we are allowed to use our free will and best judgment, not as the dominated participant. The archetype of the Queen demands that we be equal partners in all that we do.

To finish this subject on a more hopeful note, Western culture has moved more closely toward the partnership model in the past few centuries. To quote climate researcher Malcolm Hollick, Ph.D., in an article on AuthorsDen.com:

> We are no longer at the mercy of despotic kings, infallible religious authorities or the Inquisition. We no longer risk execution or burning at the stake for daring to speak out. Rape, torture, and slavery are increasingly repugnant to us. We no longer exclude women from political participation and education and reject domestic violence as wrong. We take for granted our right to vote, freedom of speech, safe working conditions, free education, desegregation, gay rights, and other gains. Our relationship with nature is becoming less abusive.

Depth psychologist and cosmologist, Richard Tarnas, offers a hopeful take on the transition from the patriarchy to a more feminine viewpoint: "The patriarchy is the 5,000-year-old birth canal of the Great Mother. We are coming into a new awareness." The emergence of the Queen archetype demonstrates the freedom modern women enjoy and the potential of a woman's psyche at midlife and beyond.

The Shadow Queen in the Patriarchy

As you'll recall, in depth psychology the *shadow* is the term for the unwanted, rejected aspects of any entity, be it a person or an archetype, such as the Queen. These aspects may be seen as negative, or they may simply have been rejected because they were not welcomed by the community (the family, religion, culture, etc.). An example might be a woman who as a child was very exuberant and expressive. In her family, these qualities were considered unseemly and unfeminine, and as a result, she was strongly encouraged to repress them. In other words, much shadow material will be judged as negative or undesirable, but it is not a given.

Any woman at midlife wanting to invite the positive queen archetype into her psyche has already found and dealt with her own wounds by having done her own psychological work either through therapy and/or analysis or assiduous self-examination with increasing personal awareness prompted by her own responses to her own life's challenges and experiences and is now able to refrain from inflicting her own unhealed wounds on others. For embodiment of the Queen to occur, she must have consciously identified her shadow and integrated it, knowing that without this awareness and composure, she might unconsciously exhibit some unwanted traits of the Queen.

The Queen is an archetype associated with personal power; therefore it follows that her negative side would involve the misuse of power. In the last chapter, we studied the Queen in her most elevated evolvement, as a beneficent, kind, caring, not self-serving woman with a broad vision for her family or community—for her realm. What would she look like if she were not any of those things? She might misuse her power by demanding that she get her way instead of winning others over to her point of view or persuading them to meet her halfway. She could be inflated—convinced that she is right in all matters because she has reached a certain point or station in her life. She might be shortsighted and only looking at the quick fix or short-term gain.

If a woman has not done enough inner work, particularly on her *animus*, the contrasexual, or masculine, aspects of her psyche (which we may term her inner masculine), she may deny the wisdom and efficacy of her internal feminine perspective or use harsher tactics than necessary to get her way. She could lose her beneficence and become a tyrant. A woman could become a Devouring Queen, who takes for her own exclusive gain and holds the reins tightly, using her power to manipulate others. Or she could become the Inflated Queen, who revels in her own exalted status and never uplifts others. That's how the shadow can play out in the real world.

Negative Queens in Popular Culture

As we all know, popular culture mirrors the ways the collective regards and values whatever is being considered. If we want to see how well or poorly the archetype of the Queen is valued, and which of her qualities we fear could be corrupted, we have only to look at the ways in which her shadow is perceived. In the case of the Queen, the culture fears a misuse of power.

Prime examples of the Negative Queen in contemporary pop culture are evident in the portrayals of older, powerful women in Disney's animated feature films. Meet the Villainesses! There's the Evil Queen from *Snow White*; Lady Tremaine, *Cinderella*'s stepmother; Ursula, Ariel's nemesis in *The Little Mermaid; 101 Dalmatians'* Cruella DeVil; and the title character in the live action film, *Maleficent*. The most recent of these villainesses, Maleficent is the only bad lady with a back-story to explain her behavior: Someone she trusted and loved stole her most precious possession, her wings, but left her other awesome powers. Maleficent wingless is still the Mistress of All Evil.

These powerful cultural depictions show how feared older women often are. Maleficent is an exception. She is not old, and is beautiful in a strong, dark way, but her powers have been compromised with the loss of her wings. The others are old with traces of their former beauty but are not *doable* in a sexual way. There is even a bit of gender bending among them, with Ursula looking like she was based on the drag queen Divine. (She was.) The take-away message is this: To be powerful, you cannot also be desirable and young. And maybe you cannot even be female. And the inverse is true too: To remain desirable, you cannot become too powerful.

Romance novelist Selene Grace Silver makes an interesting point in a blog post, entitled "Witches: The Classic Archetype of Feminine Power."

We see the evil queen carrying her basket of poisoned apples to innocent Snow White. We see the Wicked Witch of the West flying on her broomstick, with her winged monkeys, chasing Dorothy and her friends, the Tin Man, the Cowardly Lion, Scarecrow, and little Toto. We see the squinty-eyed old woman of "Hansel and Gretel" heating up her black oven, preparing to eat the candy-fattened children.

We see the negative, desperate, rejected vision of how a woman can end up: ugly, lonely, bitter. These images of the witch, multiplied and repeated from fairy tales to children's animated movies are a warning to girls: don't cultivate and express your individual power or this is what you will become.

Another example of how witches are used in our popular culture is that they are a "safe" way to show women of power. It seems television (and some movies) don't think the world is ready for the depiction of acceptable women being powerful. So, when a powerful female character is called for, she can safely be depicted as a variant of the witch: old or ugly, dark, and very scary. Anything but sexually desirable. She veers toward the dark side of the Crone.

Finding and Using Your Queenly Power

Due to living in a patriarchal society, we may have had many experiences that led us to believe that our personal power is limited. We may have been unwittingly compliant in giving our power away. Often women do that to keep the peace or for what they perceive is the greater good. If you look deeply at these reasons, you might see that we have used some of our most valuable feminine attributes to distance ourselves from our power. The beliefs engendering this behavior are that keeping the peace equals harmony and putting others before ourselves equals greater good. Or we may have gravitated toward the embodiment of masculine traits in order not to be taken advantage of by anyone.

If either case is true for you, I hope that by now you feel deeply committed to reconnecting to your personal power, so you may to make a full contribution to our world and to those you love who are living in that world. Reclaiming your personal power, as with all changes women seek to make, usually starts with taking a personal inventory. Our conscious-raising sisters of the 1960s did this, as did the suffragettes of the late nineteenth and early twentieth centuries. This is done to make ourselves aware. This important inner work needs to be done through therapy, analysis, or rigorous self-evaluation.

To heal the wounded female psyche, we must be able to see where in our lives we have become limited. Some areas of limitation might be obvious, such as governmental or religious impingement on women's rights to make decisions for our own bodies. Or limitation might show up in much subtler ways, such as in making decisions within our own families that favor our sons over our daughters, believing "the girls will have men to provide for them."

The only way you will become a Queen in your own life is first to do the inner work that a Queen needs to do. Become clear about your problems and your strengths and work to change the problematic beliefs and circumstances to foster your own awareness and clarity. Once you have cultivated your vision of how you want your life to be, then comes the work to bring in the energy of the Queen. In other words, once you have recognized the archetype and have seen how the Queen potentially could manifest in your life, it's time to issue the invitation.

In Part Two, we will explore practical steps you can take to help you ascend into your own Queenhood and make the contributions you have dreamed of to your community and your family, and, even to the world family. I have staged these as a discovery process borrowing from ancient Eastern knowledge related to the practice of yoga, of the seven chakras, which encompasses the realms of mind, body, emotions, and spirit.

PART TWO:

HOW TO EMBODY THE QUEEN

In Part Two, we will discuss the qualities of the Queen archetype and how you can begin to embody them more fully by seeing the Queen through the lens of the chakra system. Over the years, I have found that the Jungian archetypes have natural homes within the chakra system. With its origins in the ancient esoteric traditions of India—Hinduism, Buddhism, and Jainism—this system conceives of energy centers in the body as focal points for different psychological issues in our lives.

In the chapters that follow, we will explore basic information about the primary seven chakras in a woman's body, one by one, considering how they affect us physically, mentally, and emotionally, as well as how we can use our knowledge of them to integrate the Queen archetype into our daily activities and embrace our potential at midlife and beyond. I have also included a chapter on designing rituals to explore and celebrate her further. Together, these nine chapters may be considered a workbook that you can return to again and again if you wish to explore your psyche or feel that your energy has become unbalanced in some manner.

Sometimes one or another level of our being feels stagnant or blocked. Other times, one or another level of our beings feels overstimulated or flooded. The chakra system can be used as a self-analytical tool to determine where to focus on healing and personal growth. As a therapist, I believe in the power of inner work to integrate our conscious and unconscious minds and evolve throughout every stage of life. Aging is an opportunity to know ourselves better and explore the wisdom which our life experiences has gifted us.

Before we continue, let's ask and answer the most fundamental question. What is a chakra? According to ancient Hindu tradition, the subtle body, also known as the energetic body, has distribution points to transmit its energy to the physical body (see the illustration below). These energy centers are the chakras. The bioenergy of the subtle body brings function to specific parts of the physical body and provides a place for the major physical and emotional components of human life.

Although there may be an uncounted number of chakras in the body, the most commonly held belief is that there are seven main "wheels" of energy located vertically through the center of the body, and that each of these corresponds to certain states of awareness. It is these seven that we will examine to find the Queen reflected within.

Embodying the Queen energy is like orienting ourselves to the North Star. We don't expect to get there, but we can use it as a guide for how to live and stay on course.

Our chakras can be overactive, underactive, or balanced. Our aim, of course, is to have the chakras balanced. There are several ways to balance the subtle energy of our chakras. Kundalini yoga is one modality I have used to become aware and learn to work with the chakra system. Consulting an energy worker to help with this effort is also an excellent way to find and maintain your balance. Psychologically speaking, writing in a journal, meditation, and active imagination exercises are most valuable. I've included exercises like these at the end of each of the chakra chapters. Doing rituals and nurturing yourself daily also can help.

An easy way to sense the location and direction of movement is by using a pendulum. A pendulum can be made of different materials. You could use a manufactured metal pendulum, that is a weighted object that narrows to a point on one end and hangs from a flexible chain. If an "official" pendulum like this is not available, you could use a necklace of approximately six inches in length that has a simple charm or crystal on it; so long as the object weighs less than half an ounce, it should work properly for this technique. Holding a pendulum over each chakra to feel its energy, movement, and direction is an exploration that is easily done on your own.

Although it is not necessary to find your chakras with a pendulum, I feel it is most helpful to actually feel the movement of your own energy centers. Feeling the pendulum being moved by the chakra energy is a real and physical experience and doing this exploration helps you see how real this energy is.

How to Sense Your Chakras with a Pendulum

If you want to try this yourself, lie down comfortably on a sofa, a bed, or the floor. If you are familiar with pendulum work, great! If not, that's okay. It's easy to learn and fun. Hold the string or chain of the pendulum in your dominant hand, between your thumb and forefinger. In other types of pendulum work you would put your elbow on a steady surface and allow the pendulum to hang easily from your fingers with the point facing toward a table or another surface. But when doing this for yourself to locate chakras on your own body, hold the pendulum over the area where you believe the chakra is located. (Use the illustration of the chakras from page 38 for guidance.) Try to hold the pendulum as steadily as possible. If the pendulum is swinging before you begin, steady it with your other hand and then release it.

Move your hand holding the pendulum slowly over the chakra area. At some point you can expect to feel a "pull." Bring the pendulum into the center of this pull. As you do, you should start to notice the pendulum moving in a circular direction. Be patient if it doesn't happen right away. As the pendulum begins to rotate, pay attention to the direction of the circling, clockwise or counterclockwise, and the speed. Clockwise indicates the chakra is open. Counterclockwise, it is closed or blocked.

Note that the idea of clockwise is from the point of view inside your body—not from the point of view of a bodyworker or healer. When I say clockwise, I am referring to a circle that moves from your head to your right, then down toward your feet and back up to your left.

The speed or force of the rotation of the pendulum will indicate if the chakra energy is strong or weak. Do this for each of the other six chakras. When complete, go back to the closed, weak or blocked chakras, and holding your dominant hand over the chakra (you will have put the pendulum down), begin to pump up and down as if you were pushing air into that area. Do this for as long as it feels right. You can then retest that chakra and you should get a pendulum reading that shows it to be rotating strongly clockwise. If not, repeat the process.

There are other methods I have heard of for balancing the chakras, such as Reiki healing. Or you could even just ask the body to correct the closed or unbalanced chakras. If you want to take this further, play with different ways to see what works best for you.

Many spiritual modalities share similar concepts of energy. While the Hindus call subtle energy *prana*, the Chinese refer to it as *chi* or *qi*. For our purposes, it does not matter what you call it. It is your essential life force without which you could not embody the Queen.

CHAPTER 3

THE QUEEN'S FIRST CHAKRA: HER FOUNDATION OF SUPPORT

The first chakra is located at in the area between the rectum and the genitals at the perineum. In Sanskrit, it is known as the *muladhara,* a term that is derived from the words *mula,* meaning "root" and *adhara,* meaning "support." This energy center regulates our fundamental connection to the physical earth and our physical bodies, and how safe and secure we feel. It also governs our sense of identity, such as whether we see ourselves as belonging to a family, an ethnicity, and a nationality. In regulating a woman's body, it governs survival and the means to achieve it: intangible resources like money, and physical resources like food. In regulating her identity, it governs whether she feels consistently supported. The negative side of the first chakra is a constellation of thoughts, feelings, and behavior patterns that are rooted in fear.

What does the presence of the Queen in the first chakra look like in an ordinary woman's life? If you are embodying the Queen, you likely recycle everything you possibly can and run a sustainable household. You make a point to eat nutritious food and understand the importance of getting enough sleep to maintain optimum wellness. In addition, you do your best to have conscious, mutual relationships with people in any of the domains where you operate. You have a sense of abundance, grounded in good stewardship of the resources that you know you possess. You avoid taking unjustified risks and never use your personal power to gratify your ego or dominate.

The Empowered Queen vs. the Disempowered Queen

Each of the characteristics that a Queen embodies on the level of the first chakra contributes significantly to her physical and emotional sense of safety, and psychologically her sense of belonging, and of being at home in her own skin or within her family and community. When her first chakra energy is flowing and balanced, the Queen is a benevolent force for good. When her first chakra energy is stagnant and blocked or overactive, she may be arrogant, dominating, or capricious—trying to compensate for underlying fear for her very survival that likely have been with her for her entire life. Having reached midlife, the Shadow Queen may now feel threatened by her aging body or a potential loss of status, which she perceives as "dethronement."

Ambika Wauters, in her book *Chakras and Their Archetypes* describes the disempowered side of the first chakra archetype as the Victim. She describes the Victim as follows:

> The lowest level of energy and awareness is the Victim archetype. The Victim experiences itself at the mercy of outside forces which work against it. It seldom has awareness of a sense of responsibility for its circumstances. The Victim feels that "something happened to me."
>
> Victims suffer because, it appears to them, all choice has been taken from them and their fate is completely outside their control. The Victim archetype is a helpless state, totally reliant on the external world represented by a partner, companion, family, group of people or an organization, and disconnected from their inner core of feelings. The Victim's mind is stuck in a frozen state of fear, terror or desperation, with no sense of empowerment.

Having reached the stage of psychological development following the Mother, the woman who chooses to become a Queen retains all the abilities and consciousness of a Mother, but her domain is broader and her perspective higher. If she fears making this transition, such as she might when her grown children leave home and her authority over them lessens, it is important for her to reexamine how she defines herself. The woman who does not belong or feels unsafe may become the Disempowered Queen.

Reflecting on my own life and how, as a new therapist who wanted to work with older women to help them access the Crone archetype, I found such reluctance from them to accept the Crone when they were in their fifties and sixties. Because they knew that the Crone did not fit them or their lifestyles yet, I sensed intuitively that there was a missing element in the Maiden-Mother-Crone paradigm. I have to admit that my first observations of the Queen were intellectual. It took several years for me to truly grasp and fully embody the Queen in appropriate circumstances. The truth is that we all rotate roles and archetypes, embodying those in any given moment that suit our needs. The Queen archetype is powerful and compassionate, and she is never a victim, so you can call upon her when you feel you need more power to live.

Since a real-life Queen, by her very nature, is a symbol of her homeland to her subjects, the woman who embodies this archetype is someone who capable of giving others a sense of belonging, or of helping them sense that they are in their rightful places. She is a woman who understands her personal power, and she may also have a leadership role. The Queen sees money, assets, and personal wealth as the means to live a rich and fulfilling life, in which abundance contributes to how well and easily promise and potential come to fruition.

The first chakra is the source of the generativity: It helps women tap into in their roles as procreators, both as the mothers of the next generation and as creators within their professions. When women transition from the Mother archetype to the Queen, their generativity emanates from the idea of being the "mother of us all." (*Us* referring to whatever tribe or family unit the Queen belongs to.) The Empowered Queen mothers herself and her people from a psychological and emotional foundation of safety rather than from fear or a posture of victimhood.

Being Rooted in Earth

As it is with most endeavors, building a strong foundation to support that which is to be held up is the priority. So it is here. The first chakra roots us to the earth where it is essential we be tethered so as not to float off into the ethers. The Queen will sink her first chakra energy deeply into the earth, assuring her of a secure base. You may visualize this by seeing a strong, thick, well-developed root going from between the legs deep down into the earth. In your visualization, you might see this secure Earth tie, as well as the head which includes the sixth and seventh chakras now fully supported, to have the head in the upper celestial regions. Just as in gardening, the roots must be established before the flowers can bloom.

A woman who embodies the Queen holds the primary maternal energy in her social group. Her domain is not just her own physical offspring or offspring belonging to her extended family; it also extends to the immature, the yet unformed, and the powerless found in all the Earth's kingdoms. She is the mother of all creatures and creations, and her protection and beneficence provide them with a safe place to grow into their full potentials.

Being Confident in Your Body

As the Queen, you would be aware of your ability and accept your responsibility to care for all the parts of yourself. You would take care of your health and monitor your physical limits so that you could remain physically able to fulfill your leadership role, as well as to live vibrantly.

This kind of self-care can extend to even the most mundane situations. For instance, as the Queen you would be aware of how important it is to maintain good posture. You know that keeping your spine straight and supporting your back affects your ability to work well and for longer periods. Therefore, you would make sure that you have an ergonomically designed desk chair and other accessories which will add to your comfort and productivity.

By the way, you would do the same for others in your social groups who need or can benefit from mothering or nurturing leadership. You might ask for compliance with policies in your workplace that ensure the physical wellbeing and safety of those you supervise.

Belonging to a Tribe

As the Queen, you would be aware that knowing about your own ancestors has helped you form a confident personal identity. You would take comfort from knowing the strengths of the people whose genetic makeup you share. You would also understand that passing that knowledge on to your descendants or members of younger generations could help them deepen their understanding and respect for their own histories. At home, this could lead you to make efforts to instill your children and grandchildren with a love of country that would help them find and respect their national identity. You might choose to teach youth in your community about their ethnic histories, so they can develop pride in who they are and where their forbearers came from.

Alice, a divorced mother in her late forties with three adolescent children, is a good example of mothering from the level of the Queen. Alice joined Ancestry.com on a whim and began searching her own family tree. As her interest grew, she realized she wanted to share this information with her children and added the information of their father's family tree. She found it fascinating to see where both families had come from and what their ancestors had endured and accomplished. Alice talked to some of her still-living elders and heard and recorded their stories as well. As her interest in genealogy and her research skills increased, she found even more information. Ultimately, she compiled it into a drawing of a family tree with a written account that she shared with her children and extended family.

With the Queen archetype at work in her first chakra, giving a sense of belonging, Alice helped her family members develop fuller senses of where they came from and in what unique way they themselves had contributed to the greater human family story.

At age fifty-four, Jeanine, a Jewish mother of an adult daughter, had a different approach to exploring her connection with her tribe. As a former college history major, she had never lost her fascination with learning the underlying causes of modern history. For example, she often reflected on how her ancestors had come to North America and the conditions or world events, such as religious persecution, famine, or lack of economic opportunity, that led to their decisions to leave their countries of origin, separating from their families to travel halfway around the world and settle in the United States. She understood that world history was just a much larger, more complex version of an unlimited number of family stories.

In the way of a Queen, Jeanine helped her family (the *subjects* of her *realm)* recognize their lives within the context of this larger perspective. In the process, she gave her family a more detailed outlook from which to view the tapestry of history and their place within it.

Because of how Jeanine made her aware of her ancestors' courage and resilience as immigrants, whenever her daughter, Deborah, found herself being overwhelmed by obligations, such as undertaking graduate studies while caring for her two-year-old son and being a good partner to her husband, Deborah often buoyed her spirits and resolve by thinking about how the blood of her great-grandmother ran through her veins. Her great-grandmother had been a powerful matriarch who nursed a sick husband, cared for nine children, and ran a large and demanding household without falling apart. Seeing herself as a true descendant of this strong, capable woman, Deborah felt grateful that her mother had endowed her with a sense of connection to her ancestors and that she could call upon this awareness to renew her faith in herself and her abilities when times were tough. That gratitude bonded her to Jeanine.

If you are working on embodying the Queen archetype, try researching family traditions and then conveying your discoveries to members of younger generations. By being the conduit of history, traditions are preserved and passed along, increasing everyone's sense of belonging.

Playing a Leadership Role

For the woman who may not have spent her life strongly connected to family, but whose "child" has been her own professional skills, her career, or a business she owns, embodying the Queen in the first chakra might look somewhat like my friend Stephanie.

Stephanie has been a successful book editor for over thirty years. Throughout her career, she has cultivated skills for supporting writers to realize the best of their creative potential by helping them "birth" their printed children. She used Mother energy as the source for nurturing her individual clients to realize their goals of writing polished books, and she is pleased with how she has been able to contribute to various authors' successes and explorations over the years. Now at midlife, Stephanie has chosen to invite in the Queen energy. She aims to increase her public influence and has committed herself to expressing her voice in a variety of venues, from a dais, on camera, and in print. On the level of her first chakra, this transition may mean shifting her identity from being a motherly figure to a leader of a creative movement.

Remember that inviting the Queen requires us to make a choice to shift our perspective to encompass a higher, broader view, unlike the other developmental stages a woman experiences where archetypal energy comes in because of age-related shifts in her life. So, how will it be different for Stephanie to continue doing much the same work as she has done for the last twenty years while embodying the first chakra consciousness of the Queen? Stephanie plans to continue her work as an editor and publishing consultant, while adding other ventures to her activities. In this way, she hopes to contribute insights and wisdom for the greater good.

Stephanie sees her authors in a different light than she once did. She has a greater awareness of the abilities and resources each author brings and views helping them realize how they can best summon and implement their talents and minimize their challenges as fostering change on a grassroots level of cultural engagement. In addition to this high-minded purpose, Stephanie has accrued a broad understanding of publishing as a business. She knows what sells, and to whom it sells. She sees what kinds of books are selling and what publishers are looking for in those books. Her overview of the publishing field, coupled with her highly skilled editing, are allowing her to work at that higher level we have noted in a worldly queen— that of seeing what the needs of a community are and what resources she might allocate to that need. She even uses her Queen energy to protect and nurture immature and unformed "beings," such as books, that are being prepared for publishing. She holds space for ideas to develop.

As a Queen, in the workplace you may decide you want to mentor someone. The relationship of mentor to mentee is another of those nurturing roles that a woman at the apex of her career may choose. She may see an employee whose skills are primarily good, but still need refinement and polishing. By taking on a mutually agreed upon mentoring arrangement, she can help her mentee polish the rough spots and learn a few useful tricks. A successful mentoring relationship can make the difference between success and failure for the mentee, as well as allowing a Queen to help one of her own move forward.

Being a Good Steward of Your Resources, Money, and Possessions

Since first-chakra consciousness is concerned with the basic means for physical survival in the world, including the need for food, shelter, and clothing, and the means to purchase, procure, and keep safe all that is necessary for physical survival for members of the Queen's realm, issues of career and money management play a spotlight role in the life of every woman who embodies the Queen. Money gives her access to resources, and thereby, control over her fate.

One of the most important responsibilities of a worldly Queen is the procurement and the management and allocation of resources. As the Queen, to rule your dominion judiciously, you must be aware of where needs are the greatest and where the resources to respond to those needs are to be found. You are the one responsible for seeing that there are adequate means to fund daily activities and maintain the lifestyle of your subjects, and to plan for a secure future.

A woman living within this archetype has many responsibilities and opportunities. As the Queen, it may not necessarily be your primary or exclusive responsibility to oversee the income and outgo in your household, for instance because you may have a partner or spouse heading the household alongside you. However, any woman who is charged with being a leader at home would do well to approach this area of responsibility with the enlightenment that the Queen archetype brings. A head of household needs to have the mature wisdom to discern where the greatest needs and potentials are and direct resources there on a timely basis.

If she is effective, the matriarch of a large family is aware of what's going on in the lives of each of the members of her family; she knows what their needs are, as well as their hopes and dreams. By using her knowledge and influence judiciously, she can direct the resources under her control in a way that brings the greatest good to the largest number of family members.

For instance, a woman working within the Queen archetype might be aware that her son and his wife are very anxious to have a home of their own and stop renting. They want to feel settled, have a place to raise their children, and build equity. But today's high qualifications for a mortgage and down payment are slowing them down considerably. So, the mother, embodying the Queen Archetype with her higher perspective, looks for a way she may be able to help them. Realizing that the lake cabin where they often spent their summers is no longer being used much, she makes an offer to her son and his wife. "Help me get the cabin cleaned up and do some of the long-needed repairs and we'll put it on the market. You both will get the proceeds of the sale, which should be more than enough for your down payment." In this instance she is operating like a wise and beneficent monarch, and by having an overview that others may not be able to have, she can operate wisely.

Let's look at one more example of how Queen energy might manifest itself on the first-chakra level through a woman's management of money and resources.

Linda is a sixty-year-old lesbian. She has had several long-term relationships, some more fulfilling than others with none lasting longer than five years. When Linda was younger, she often thought how much she would like to have a child, but the idea of raising a child alone seemed daunting, so she put away whatever thoughts she had of motherhood and in a few years turned her attention instead to the care of her now chronically ill mother and to holding down her full-time job as a bookkeeper. In the four-year period after her mother's death, she began feeling an emptiness that seemed to go beyond the grief she experienced from the loss of her mother. Because of her sense of emptiness, she decided to make a professional change. She took a job as an administrative assistant at a non-profit agency that served gay, lesbian, bisexual, and transgender youth, as well as men and women in the LGBT community.

As an administrative assistant, Linda wore many hats—the usual administrative duties, from events planner, to project coordinator for the agency's events, chief cook, and bottle washer. An unexpected source of joy in her new job came from spending time with the kids who came to the Center nearly every day. Most of these kids had experienced unstable home lives and had not been loved or accepted by their families and had little or no support. Linda's loving acceptance of them and her emotional awareness of how difficult their lives had been, afforded an instant bond between them. Linda's presently unused nurturing abilities were reawakened. These were feelings that had not been used since her mother's passing.

Because Linda held a seat on the agency's board of directors, she had been made aware of scholarships for students from the LGBT community. One of the kids with whom Linda had made a particularly strong connection fit many of the criteria this scholarship required. Like the true Queen she has become, Linda was able to help one of her "kids" apply for and get this scholarship. Linda, under the Queen Archetype, made the connection that nurtured a child, (an unformed, immature being), found an unmet need of that child, and was in the position to be aware of an important resource and that then helped that child realize her potential.

So, how do you bring Queen energy into the areas of your life that are governed by your first chakra? Recognize that functioning as a Queen requires a broadening of your perspective. Use the following exercises to help you sense the presence of the Queen archetype.

Meeting the Queen in Your First Chakra

Think of the areas in your life that the first chakra influences: health, personal identity, safety, belonging, or resources. Choose a situation in your life that fits into one of these areas. This is a good time to consider the different social spheres of which you are a part. I suggest that you write them down on paper. The categories may be as simple as: Home, Work, School, Volunteer Position, Church/Synagogue, and the name of a club you belong to. Or you could be more detailed. You may be surprised at how many people's lives intersect with your own.

Once you have selected a first-chakra issue to work with, do your best to think of all the ways you might solve or resolve this issue for yourself. While doing this, allow yourself to go into a relaxed, contemplative state. At this point, imagine the Queen archetype (in whatever way your imagination works), and ask her to grace you with her presence while you are thinking about her qualities.

Once you have invited the Queen to work through you, feel yourself expanding your perspective on the situation, seeing it from a higher level. Hold this new perspective for as long as you can, feeling the Queen inspire you.

Then go back to your situation and review it as the Queen.

An example, it might be that you do not feel you belong. It might be a lifelong experience or a temporary, circumstantial one. As you follow the instructions written above, your sense of disconnection begins to shift towards sure recognition that you have always belonged, because, as a Queen, you have the right to belong.

You have the power to make the rules for yourself and they are as valid as any rules meant to exclude you. It is by this new awareness of who you are becoming that you open the door to this archetypal energy.

You could also practice thinking of how the Queen might be, or act, in your own everyday situations, such as grocery shopping, at the gym, riding the bus, or preparing dinner. (I know there is a humorous aspect to imaging a Queen at the gym, doing reps!) It is best to do this imaging while you are performing these activities.

Journaling About the Queen

You will need paper and a pen to complete this exercise. Or you can park yourself in front of your laptop. Just be sure you are comfortably seated and somewhere you won't be disrupted.

Think of any situation in your life where a first chakra quality is problematic for you. When you find one you would like to focus on, take some time to imagine several ways you might possibly solve or resolve this problem.

You have decided you want to further build your financial nest egg by investing in the stock market. It feels intimidating to you to do this. You have heard that you need to know about the companies you invest in, have a good stock broker, be gifted with knowing the right time to buy and, even more importantly, the right time to sell. It all feels somewhat overwhelming and a potentially risky place to put your hard-earned money.

Now, ask the Queen to show herself to your mind's eye. What do see first about her? Flesh her out. See her in detail. What is she wearing? Perhaps you will see her arrayed in a shade of red, the color for this chakra. What does her crown look like? Her crown maybe a twigs of wood, recalling that this first chakra is strongly related to to the earth. Mentally ask her to help you clarify the image. Feel yourself expanding and growing, still seeing your problem, although from a higher perspective. Hold this for as long as you can, asking the Queen to help you see the issue from this higher vantage point.

Then go back to looking at your situation and review it as the Queen. Embody her. If you are following the instructions written above, your sense of overwhelm will begin to shift toward the sure recognition that you have always known that you have the gift of wealth, because as a Queen, wealth and security are integral to your station as a Queen. You will see that you have the power to look at financial situations and interpret the information, and, if still unsure, like a good Queen, you will consult with your advisors. This could mean finding a good stockbroker or financial consultant to help educate yourself and make wise decisions.

It is with this new awareness of who you are becoming that you open the door to this archetypal energy and the possibilities for the resolution of your issues.

When you feel you have clarity on this first chakra issue, open your eyes and write in your journal. Describe everything you saw, heard, felt, and understood. Write in a stream of consciousness without censorship. Let the Queen speak on the page if she wants to. Let this be a sacred, regal experience of beautiful self-connection. An act of self-love.

First Chakra Meditation

Another way to meet the Queen is in a meditation.

Find a quiet place where you won't be disturbed for ten to fifteen minutes. Turn off your smartphone, or better yet, leave it somewhere where you won't be tempted to look at it, like inside a drawer or in another room. Make yourself comfortable either in a chair or lying down.

If you choose to do this seated, it is best to sit in a chair that supports your spine, so you can easily maintain your upright position. (An erect spine facilitates the movement of energy in your body.) Place your feet flat on the floor and rest your hands comfortably in your lap or on the tops of your thighs.

If you choose to do this lying down, you may wish to put a bolster or cushion under your knees to reduce the strain on your lower back. Let your arms rest comfortably near your sides. This is the position in yoga known as Corpse Pose *or Sivasana.*

You may want to cover yourself with a light blanket or throw. Turn the lights down or off. The idea is to create a comfortable, quiet space where you are not likely to be disturbed.

Begin by closing your eyes and taking a deep breath. Breathe as deeply as you can without forcing, inhaling through the nose and exhaling through the mouth. Do this for four or five breaths, and then begin to exhale through your nose. Pay attention to the pattern of your breathing, and the movement of air in and out through your nose, until you feel yourself start to relax.

Now, to deepen your sense of relaxation, concentrate on your feet. Notice if they feel achy or tense. With your next inhalation, imagine you are sending a feeling of softness and warmth all the way down to your feet and toes. (Don't worry if you have not done this before, it gets easier with practice. Sometimes just the attempt is enough to start the relaxation process.) You can mentally send your breath to your feet several times if you wish.

Then, when you are ready, with the next inhalation, imagine you are sending the breath down to your lower legs, feeling them being covered with warm softness, like a soft fuzzy blanket just out of the dryer. Feel the tension in your calf muscles release and notice them becoming softer and less rigid. Bring the warmth from your calves up into your thighs and feel your powerful quadriceps and hamstring muscles letting go and relax.

Again, when you are ready, allow the soft, caressing warmth you sense in your legs to move up into your lower torso, both front and back, and feel all the tension leaving your lower abdomen, your buttocks, and lower back. Take a moment to really enjoy the sensations of warmth and relaxation.

Now, feel the warmth spread further up your body to the chest and the midback, loosening any tightness that you find there. Focus again for a moment on your breathing as your chest relaxes more and your breathing becomes easier and deeper.

Now, bring the soft warmth all the way up your torso to your shoulders. After a moment or two of relaxing with this focus, check back on the rest of your body. It should feel much more relaxed than when you started. If you notice a place or two that still feels tense, send your next outbreath to those spots.

When you feel that you have reached a good state of relaxation, begin to imagine the warmth moving up your neck, both front and back, loosening the neck muscles, which often hold a great deal of tension. You may want to take some extra time here if you encounter significant tension.

Allow the warmth now to move up the back of your head, covering your entire skull. I often imagine this feeling as a sensation like covering my head with a baby's bonnet. Let the warmth then begin to travel down your forehead, smoothing and soothing it. The warmth can then move further down your face, all the way to the jawline.

You may want to pay special attention to the place where your jaw hinges, your temporomandibular joint (TMJ). That is another place you may hold tension.

You have now completely relaxed your body. Don't worry if you think it isn't good enough. It most likely is and you will become better at relaxing each time you go through this process.

Once you are feeling very relaxed, ask the Queen to appear to you in your mind's eye. Because you are working with the first chakra, you may want to visualize her with attributes of that chakra. You may see her as a tall and sturdy tree trunk, with well-developed roots that sinking deeply into the earth. You may see her wearing a beautiful red robe, as red is the color that corresponds to the first chakra. At her feet are all the necessities for life here on Earth, such as cornucopias filled with life giving food, or piles of coins, signifying wealth. Behind her there may be rows and rows of her ancestors, stretching back as far as you can see. In front of her may be two or three rows of her descendants, the fruits of her body or the results of her labors.

This is your meditation, so feel free to imagine the Queen in the way that most reflects who you are as a person. You may visualize her with a beautiful golden crown on her head. You may see her being surrounded by a radiance of vitality and good health. Let her face hold an expression of serenity, acknowledging her sense of security in who she is and what she has.

Take time to embellish your vision of her adding whatever details seem to belong. As you do this, your first chakra Queen will become more alive to you.

Then, as you continue to hold your vision of her, see the Queen beckon to you. Imagine yourself walking toward her as she gently takes your hand. Ask her to bless you with her abundant, strong presence, and to endow you with all the qualities she represents. See her putting her hand on your head and feel the strength of her energy enter your body.

Spend a moment on this, letting yourself really *feel* it. Let Queen energy move down through your body to your first chakra from the crown of your head, and then let it flow all the way down to your feet. Imagine your feet beginning to grow roots. Let these roots grow long and thick as they sink down into the earth under your feet and root you strongly in ground. Take a minute or two to let this happen. When the visualization feels complete, thank your Queen for her blessings and support and allow your image of her to fade.

As you continue your deep, relaxed breathing, feel yourself returning to everyday awareness. Without rushing, when you are ready, open your eyes, rub the palms of your hands and the soles of your feet together to bring yourself fully back into your physical reality. When you feel fully alert, you may return to your daily activities, knowing that you have done something wonderful and healing for yourself.

Active Imagination

Another way to more fully get to know your Queen as you see her in your first chakra is to use the Jungian tool of *active imagination*. This can be thought of as an exchange conducted by you with any imagined or real entity in your life. The invitation and intention is to access your unconscious mind, or as Carl Jung writes in his book *The Transcendent Function:* It is "for the production of those contents of the unconscious which lie, as it were, immediately below the threshold of consciousness and when intensified, are the most likely to erupt spontaneously into the conscious mind."

For this exercise, I would like to suggest that you sit in front of your computer, or if you are more comfortable with writing this out in longhand, by all means do so. As with any of these very personal exercises, approach them with reverence, both for what you are attempting and for whom you will be attempting to contact.

It will be important that you are protected from being disturbed. Find a quiet place, preferably with a door. Spend a few minutes quieting your mind, as you would do for meditation. Before beginning, decide on which of the two ways you are going to use this time. (I suggest you try them both at different times, to see which one works better for you.)

The first method is the visual method. Allow your mind to come up with a scene or an image that has meaning for you. It could come from a recent dream, or from another source such as an arresting artwork you have recently seen. The essential component is that this image has a charge, a connection, for you. Close your eyes and bring this figure into sharp focus. See what that entity is wearing; see the facial expression, the hair and any accessories, such as hats, crowns, swords, scepters, baskets, etc. When you feel you have sharpened the image in your mind's eye as much as possible, hold that picture as you begin to allow the fantasy to unfold.

During the fantasy, you may ask for clarification if you're not sure of what you are seeing. You may also ask questions of your unconscious (for it is the unconscious you have engaged), regarding the meaning of a chosen component of the fantasy. The magic happens when you find yourself moving back and forth between observing and interacting with the unconscious material.

When you have taken this as far as you find comfortable, you may end the exercise by thanking the unconscious for being available, and then slowly, gently allowing yourself to return to normal wakefulness.

You will want to write down what you experienced, date it, and keep it either in your dream journal or a notebook for active imagination. You may want to continue working with this Active Imagination, while it is fresh, or put it away for a day or two before trying to interpret it.

The other method of doing active imagination is oral. You engage in conversation with a person or object that you intuitively feel has a bearing on the issue at hand. If you are sitting in front of your computer or writing longhand in a journal, the conversation between you and your chosen entity or the entity that appears to you can be written like a standard interview. You ask the question and wait to hear what the image responds. This is where first-time users of active imagination may have some doubts, or start to feel silly. Just tolerate the discomfort. Stick with it and you may find yourself typing or writing things that you have not consciously thought about.

If you find yourself feeling like you're "just making it up," ask yourself these questions: "Why is it this and not something else?" "Why is the Queen answering this way and not that?"

You ask the question and just write down whatever comes out. Allow that "voice" to speak as long as it will. When you feel the answer is complete, switch back into your personality and react to what has been said, asking another question, and continuing the conversation. Sometimes you don't actually hear words but find them flowing from your hands onto the keyboard or page.

With either of these methods, you might not get fully developed ideas or information. That is normal; even Carl Jung experienced this.

You can fill in some of the missing information from the feelings you are experiencing, including feelings in the body, as well as those that present in a more mental way.

Now that you have begun your internal conversation with your Inner Queen with meditation and active imagination, you can continue your converse with the Queen as you get to know her in the Second Chakra.

Summary
The Queen in the First Chakra

Below is a short list of the ways in which you can remind yourself of how the first chakra looks in a woman who embodies the Queen.

The Queen:

- Takes responsibility for the health of her body.
- Often connects with nature and views herself as a steward of the Earth.
- Cares for all forms of still growing and immature entities and provides protection for them.
- Embodies and holds for others a sense of belonging.
- Sees and uses money and other resources as the means to having possibilities become realities.
- Is able to direct resources to the needs she identifies.
- Helps others to see and appreciate the identity and history

CHAPTER 4

THE QUEEN'S SECOND CHAKRA: HER SOURCE OF CREATIVITY AND PROCREATIVITY

The second chakra, or sacral chakra, is located above the pubic bone and below the navel. Its Hindu name, *svasthana,* is derived from the Sanskrit words *swa*, meaning "one's own" and *adisthana* meaning "dwelling." This energy center is where our personal energy lives. It is associated with procreation, sexuality, and creativity. It also connects a woman with beauty, sensual pleasure, and her enjoyment of life. Within the Queen archetype, each of these qualities may be experienced as complex and interwoven, as they will be for a mature woman. The negative side of the second chakra is a constellation of thoughts, feelings, and behavior patterns that are rooted in stunted creativity, sexual dysfunction, shame, and addiction.

All archetypes have a positive and a negative side. For the second-chakra Queen, the positive side is that of the Empress and the negative side is that of the Martyr. The Empress experiences a sense of wellbeing, taking pleasure at the abundance she sees in her life. She always has a good time. The Martyr, on the other hand, has given up on her right to enjoy life and feel pleasure. She fills her days with duty, sacrifice, and lack.

Women embodying the Martyr are often encouraged by others to stay in this role, because our culture sees self-abnegation as a virtue and sacrifice as a moral position. Also, the encouragement of others is self-serving for, as it keeps Martyrs doing what they do best, which is carrying all the burdens.

Notice how these polarities are opposite sides of the same coin.

The Empress is abundant, energetic, and enjoying all the good which is in her life. The Martyr lives with a sense of scarcity. She is self-denying, joyless, and often lacking in vitality.

Procreation and Creativity

While your first chakra relates to your physical needs, your second chakra relates to your emotional reality. Its consciousness is all about desire and connection, which is one of the most emotional issues in most women's lives. Whereas the first chakra informs us what we must have, do, and be to *survive*, the second chakra informs us what we must have, do, and be to thrive and *connect*.

Women are intimate with the force of life, which is a creative force. But whether a woman has been a biological mother does not affect her overall creativity. Physical reproduction is not as relevant an issue now that she is either approaching, undergoing, or has passed through menopause. Today, women remain relevant and can be productive as long as they want to and their health will allow it. Their wisdom and leadership energy are needed.

The children of many women who embody the Queen have already left home for good or are in college and preparing to launch households of their own. These women may be in the middle of the process of redefining themselves—at least partly—outside the role of being the mom to one or more young people. Even so, they continue to create. Like raising a child to become a happy adult, producing a work of art, decorating a beautiful home, landscaping a garden, cooking a delicious meal. All are acts of creation. Every form of creativity is rooted in the energy of the second chakra.

By the time she reaches this stage of life, a woman who is ready to embody the energy of the Queen will be open to trying new things. She also may have an appreciation for doing things well and masterfully that she didn't have when she was younger and more driven by the hormones associated with reproduction. She now knows to take her time.

Creativity is one of the traits that separate us from other animals. The urge to deliberately create works of art—be they essays, novels, or poems, music, paintings, sculptures, or gorgeous cupcakes—can lift a woman's own spirits and also be used by her to raise the spirits of others. Having a strong and balanced second chakra is a foundation for healthy self-love. If her second chakra is blocked, overactive, or weakened in some way, however, a woman may not love herself enough to stand up for her needs in relationships beyond pure survival.

Grace's story illustrates how weakness in the second chakra can influence a woman's choices. Grace, in her twenties, was passionate. She cared deeply about her professional life as a dancer, inspiring the audience by dancing with heart. In her personal life, she also gave fully of herself in many ways to her husband, her friends, and her pets. But she was a born dancer. She loved using her gift both for her own pleasure and for the pleasure it brought others. As her primary form of creativity, dance illuminated her life.

Unfortunately, with rare exceptions dance doesn't bring in a significant income. And dance careers on stage are relatively brief because they are so physically demanding. Out of a misguided sense of duty, Grace put her performance dreams aside to support her husband financially while he pursued his creative goals as an actor. They agreed she would get a more conventional job as an office administrator and become the household's primary breadwinner. Although she found work that paid better than dancing did, and she was competent in her new career, it brought her much less personal satisfaction. Her job was just a paycheck.

As Grace aged and her window of opportunity to be successful as a dancer closed, she noticed a feeling of emptiness growing inside her. Years went by and she tried filling the emptiness with many things: drink, food, a short fling with drugs, and shopping, but none of these things ever healed the wounds in her damaged second chakra. Grace had done what she believed was right—sacrificing everything that made her come alive creatively for the sake of the man she loved—but she had lost touch with an essential part of herself in the bargain.

When Grace reached midlife, she was flooded with regret. She realized how much her sacrifice had cost her and how emotionally empty it had left her, she grieved for what she had abandoned. Then, embracing the wisdom of the Queen, she looked for a new way to express her talents for movement through a more meaningful occupation. She was able to reclaim her gift by becoming a dance teacher and helping young girls and boys to express themselves creatively. As she did, she felt restored and energized. She looked forward to going to work every day.

The Disempowered Queen vs. the Empowered Queen

Overeating, addictive drinking and dependence on drugs, smoking, sexual promiscuity, and compulsive shopping and gambling, are indications of disturbances in the second chakra. It's not hard to see how each of these activities and substances relates to pleasure, but in an unhealthy way—one that enslaves a woman over time and does not produce lasting pleasure.

If the work of confronting a compulsion or addiction has not yet been done, the Queen stage of life provides an opportunity for a woman to correct or redirect her second chakra energy, restoring its balance and making it available so she may use it to reach the next level in her psychological and spiritual development. One of the best ways she can do this important work is through forming a loving connection with her body.

At fifty-one, Pamela began taking yoga classes to stay limber and handle stress. When she started, reducing her stress and improving her flexibility were her only goals, and a friend recommended yoga as a good choice for her.

As a teenager and young adult, Pamela had become extremely disconnected from her body. An intellectual, she viewed her body as a nuisance. There were even times she wished she could exist only from the neck up, so she could just sit, read, and think, and not be bothered by the "troublesome" needs of her body. She was a classic type A workaholic who spent a lot of time in front of her computer at the office.

During her first yoga class, Pamela felt clumsy and found herself unable to do some of the poses, much less hold them for the allotted time. She felt as if when her brain gave an order for her arm to extend in Warrior pose, the message just wasn't getting through the way she expected. Despite this less-than-thrilling first class, Pamela noticed afterward that she felt good—in fact, very good. Her muscles had been stretched, her torso twisted, and she could immediately feel several pleasant results from her workout. Among other things, she felt light and buoyant and mentally alert.

Pamela established a yoga practice and in the intervening years became a good enough yogini to join a teacher training program. Today, Pamela cannot imagine how it used to be when she only wanted to live in her head, instead of enjoying her body through this ancient body/mind modality. Pamela has moved beyond the confines of the body disowning attitude she had that characterized her pre-yoga days, and now with her expanded awareness—from the perspective of the Queen—she enjoys her body and its responsiveness every day.

Sensuality and Sexuality

The desire to belong and connect with a partner is natural. As is the desire to recognize and respond to a partner's desire to connect with us. It feels good to connect sensually to our partners' bodies and to our own. However, none of us requires a partner to express and experience our sexuality or lead a sensual lifestyle.

As mature women embodying the Queen, we are familiar with the functions of the second chakra. Our sexual urges are not new to us. Even so, due to the biological changes associated with aging, our sexuality may express itself differently in midlife than it did in our youth. The rebalancing of our sexual hormones has not been this intense since adolescence. We get a chance to revisit and put the past behind us, and to make choices of what to do with the rest of our lives. Pleasure experienced through our senses is healing to the second chakra.

If she is to embody the Queen going forward, among other things it may be necessary for a woman to confront and heal psychological issues that have interfered or are currently interfering with her enjoyment and acceptance of her sexuality. She may need to look inward and remember life events that damaged her self-esteem or wounded her sexually, so she may find appropriate means to heal her pain and shame. Personal introspection, therapy, conversations with a good friend or mentor, and journaling are some of the means you might use to do second-chakra healing inner work.

For a woman to embody the Queen, she must be able to function at her highest level and her energy must flow freely. If she has personal blockages in her second chakra, they will need to be addressed. Too many women have been sexually abused, raped, or exploited. Often their feelings about these types of violating experience get repressed and never are given a chance to fully heal. It is hard to avoid being reminded of past trauma, given that we live in a culture which undervalues and disrespects women in many instances.

At midlife, a woman who has not yet had an opportunity to examine her psychic injuries and heal from them would do well to do inner work at midlife. Seeing a therapist for in-depth counseling to uncover how her sexuality was injured and what this has meant to her will be of primary importance. Because female sexuality is such a powerful part of us, yet makes us vulnerable, injuries of a sexual nature that go back to childhood and adolescence are particularly difficult to explore alone. Often if someone has misused a woman during childhood, that abuser will also have told her an untruth, such as "It's okay," "It's our secret," or "It's your fault, because you enjoyed it," or otherwise embedded in the woman some other confusing thoughts. Sorting out these old memories and debunking the lies leads a woman to gain a clearer perspective on her entire life.

Being sexually abused had colored Jessica's thinking and crippled her intimate relationships throughout her life. When she was no more than three or four, Jessica had been molested by an older cousin when he and her aunt had come for a visit. She felt uncomfortable, and yet excited, by what had happened, but told no one because he said not to and threatened her with harm. Over the years, every time the aunt and cousin visited again, her cousin would find a way of getting Jessica alone. His actions toward her became more sexual, and her feelings about what was happening became more charged with both excitement and dread. Jessica felt particularly bad about enjoying these encounters, but also felt special because of her cousin's attentions.

Later, as a sexually active young woman, Jessica experienced complicated feelings about wanting sex with the man who was her partner at any given time. She could sometimes enjoy making love, but the feelings of guilt she had experienced when being sexually molested by her cousin were often there, too. As the years went by, Jessica tried to understand her ambivalent feelings about sex, but because she could not find a way to enjoy sex without simultaneously experiencing guilt and confusion, she ultimately decided sex was not worth all the trouble. She shut down.

Memories of her early injuries robbed Jessica for decades of the pleasure and intimacy that were her birthright. It was only when her husband, Renaldo, threatened to end their marriage due to his frustration at not having a sexually responsive wife that Jessica began seeing a psychotherapist to find out why she was no longer interested in being intimate with him. Over time, with the support of her husband and therapist, she began to uncover the old memories of her molestation by her cousin and to release her shame.

Today, Jessica can acknowledge her pleasure and fully enjoy sexual arousal, without her desire being a dark secret that she once denied even to herself.

Psychotherapists with compassion, training, and insight can help us discover the truth about our lives, understand how we were not responsible for bad things that may have happened to us as children or as adults, and view negative experiences from a perspective that allows us to feel whole again and move forward. We also can help ourselves to heal through the ongoing use of self-care techniques like the ones you find at the end of the chapter, such as writing in a journal, meditating, and using active imagination. When the energy of the second chakra is restored to balance, we have more emotional freedom, regain energy that has been spent to suppress memory, and feel less fear related to the expression of our sexuality.

Another way in which the second chakra can be damaged is through the rejection—be it conscious or otherwise—of our attempts to connect with others and share the joy of beauty. It is certainly beautiful to watch a sunset alone, but there is almost always a wistful desire to share such transcendent experiences with another being. Can you remember ever longing to connect with someone when viewing a spectacular sunset?

Angela had many of the things she had wanted and worked for in her life. She loved her steady, dependable husband, who had fathered her three children, in a friendly, if somewhat distant way. Although for a while she had worked to bring in extra money, having reached retirement age she did not see herself as having had a career. Now that the children were launched into adulthood, she and her husband were looking at themselves and each other for the first time in many years. They shared a history and Angela was proud of the work they had done together to successfully raise their offspring. But now she was wondering what the coming years would be like.

As Angela looked over her life, she began to realize that what seemed missing was a sense of devotion, a soul-level connection, and passion. Digging deeper, she realized that although she did love her husband, Derek, and believed their love life had been adequate, she still felt that there should have been more sharing. Angela's introspection continued over some time. She began to review her history to see if she could find the source of disconnection from her spouse in her earlier life. She found that journaling was a way for her to go back in her memory and recapture past experiences.

Angela allowed herself quiet time to sit and allow old memories to come to the surface of her mind. When she did this, she became aware that some memories had a certain strong feeling to them. She followed her intuition as to which ones were important. She would then write about those memories without censoring anything and allowing whatever came up to be there.

One of the memories she wrote about was of a time as a three-year-old when she felt connected to her senses, to others, to beauty, to pleasure. She remembered an incident that happened in the spring when she had become aware of the beauty of the flowers blooming and the magic that springtime brings for the first time in her young life. She recalled being almost intoxicated by the beauty of the flowers and wanting to somehow take the beauty in. Sweetly, she decided to pick flowers from her neighbor's yard and give them to her mother. But her mother's response was not what Angela was hoping for. In fact, her mother was horrified that Angela had picked flowers belonging to the neighbor. Instead of Angela connecting with her mother in the way she desired, and instead of seeing her mother delight with her in the beauty of the flowers, she was given a lecture on why stealing was wrong and made to apologize to the neighbor.

Picking flowers was her first experience of getting in trouble for having and acting on her desires. Her second chakra took a big hit and its energy began to shut down that day in a way that had affected her throughout her life.

Angela decided to draw upon the courage of the Queen archetype to heal her past so that she could regenerate the aspect of herself that was open to pleasure and begin to form stronger, more passionate relationships. She continued to replay other memories of attempts at connection, and of connections others had forced upon her. The usual teenage heartbreaks showed up. A memory also surfaced of a male family member touching her in a way she knew was wrong. Bit by bit, Angela saw how she had been wounded in the areas the second chakra influenced.

Once Angela's journaling unearthed these painful memories and she had examined them, she was able to see them as parts of a pattern that was still active in her current life. She decided she wanted to forgive those who had caused her pain, knowing that it had not been intentional on their part, so she could finally let go of her barriers to intimacy. As she reviewed each of the memories once more, she could now compassionately see how the others' actions were prompted by misunderstandings, their own concerns, and in the case of her male relative, a mental illness, and with forgiveness, she freed up a considerable amount of psychic energy. Afterward, she felt she was now able to offer her husband and their union a fuller measure of love and devotion. Noticing the new openness in her toward him, her husband reciprocated.

Many women internalize the patriarchy's poor view of their intrinsic worth as they are growing up and feel ashamed after having been denigrated by the treatment they've received in a variety of circumstances. Having been led to believe that their desires and bodies are somehow not okay, and that feeling and seeking pleasure is not an appropriate option for them, when they reach midlife, they often find that they are finally ready to reexamine those false beliefs and replace them with loving, accepting feelings about their bodies and celebrate using their bodies for pleasurable purposes, including to express love and connection with others.

Meeting the Queen in Your Second Chakra

Now, it's time for you to explore the energy of the Queen, as you did in the last chapter, by inviting her to come through you as you go about your day, journaling about her, and meditating upon her. In all three of these exercises you will be engaging her using your imagination as we explored in the last chapter. Please experiment with the second-chakra energy of the Queen for as long as you like before moving on to read the next chapter. The following techniques can all be used to access the Queen in different ways.

Inviting the Queen to Come Through You

Because your present focus is on your second chakra, you may want to spend some time thinking about how the Queen would express herself as a creative being, perhaps through painting or writing. Imagine how pleased and fulfilled she feels when she is possessed by her muse or when her process of creation is complete. As you engage in creative actions, breathe into the area of your second chakra (between your pubic bone and your navel) and invite her to enter your body. Try being the Queen as you cook dinner tonight or while you type an office memo. How does that change your experience of what you are doing? Does it enrich the experience? And do you enjoy yourself more?

You might also imagine the Queen seeking and establishing personal connections with others, sharing their joys and sorrows with them and receiving their support and companionship. Because the Queen is a leader, does inviting her to enter your body when you are listening to a friend change the nature of your interaction? Breathe her energy into your belly. Do you feel more grounded and connected to yourself when you are asking for help to get something done? Often leaders must hold space for a weaker, or less accomplished person. Therefore, a woman has to learn to be less reactive and less egoic to be a Queen.

You might even imagine the Queen having super satisfying sex. (In my mind's eye, her crown is a little askew, her robes rumpled, but she is still a Queen. She brings all of herself to bed, and takes responsibility for her own sexual pleasure, though she is also comfortably able to give any direction needed to her partner.) See what happens when you embody the Queen in your own bedroom. Does the experience become more sensual and passionate? How has your comfort level changed? Can you allow yourself to be more vulnerable with your partner, knowing that you are stronger and less sensitive to your usually expected rejection?

Keep in mind the domains of the second chakra: creativity, sensuality, sexuality, and pleasure. Now is a wonderful time for you to heal any issues you experience in these areas of your life by drawing upon the archetypal Queen energy. She can help you transcend obstacles that once limited you and give you a new perspective.

As we did with the first chakra, you could also practice thinking of how the Queen might be, or act, in everyday second-chakra situations: See how the Queen would be in the arms of her lover, enjoying the closeness and pleasure. How would the Queen appear to you as she easily chatted with a stranger, feeling a connection forming? See the Queen signing up for that watercolor class she has wanted to take, knowing that the spark of divine inspiration is within her and its hers to express. And if you want a humorous image, how about a pregnant Queen getting a sensual massage while dictating her novel to an assistant? (It is also wonderful to do this kind of imaging while you are performing these activities.)

Journaling About the Queen

You will need paper and a pen to complete this exercise. Or you can park yourself in front of your laptop. Just be sure you are comfortably seated and somewhere you won't be disrupted.

As you did for the first chakra journaling exercise (see page 51), begin by thinking of any situation in your life where second chakra qualities are problematic for you. When you find one you would like to focus on, take some time to imagine several ways you might possibly solve or resolve this problem.

An example, you have always wanted to write a novel, and have made several attempts at starting, but you are afraid to let anyone read your manuscripts, because you don't think your writing is good enough. Let's say you often worry, *How can my work be worth the time for others to read? How can I compare myself to any of the published fiction writers out there?*

Now, ask the Queen to show herself to your mind's eye. What do see first about her? Flesh her out. See her in detail. What is she wearing? Perhaps somewhere in her raiment you will find a touch of orange. (Orange is the color associated with this chakra.) What does her crown look like? Mentally ask her to help you clarify the image. Feel yourself expanding and growing, still seeing your problem, although from a higher perspective. Hold this for as long as you can, asking the Queen to help you see the issue from this higher vantage point.

Then go back to looking at your situation and review it as the Queen. Embody her. If you are following the instructions written above, your sense of unworthiness will begin to shift toward the sure recognition that you have always known that you have the gift of storytelling, because as a Queen, your stories are worth hearing. You will see that you have the power to tell spell-binding stories from your treasure-trove of experience and imagination. Can you imagine a Queen feeling like she has no right to pursue her art? Or feeling that she has no right to express herself? Of course not.

It is with this new awareness of who you are becoming that you open the door to this archetypal energy and the possibilities for the resolution of your issues.

Let's say the situation you have chosen to work on is your difficulty in telling your lover how to please you sexually. Try and imagine the Queen being shy and reticent, unable to say what she needs. Doesn't compute, right? It's hard to imagine the Queen not taking care of her own pleasure. Would you rather be an Empress or a Martyr?

When you feel you have clarity on the second chakra issue, open your eyes and write in your journal. Describe everything you saw, heard, felt, and understood. Write in a stream of consciousness without censorship. Let the Queen speak on the page if she wants to. Let this be a sacred, regal experience of beautiful self-connection. An act of self-love.

Second Chakra Meditation

Another powerful way to invite the Queen into your second chakra is in meditation. Many women enjoying using this type of meditation to start or end their days.

For your convenience, I am repeating the following relaxation induction instructions as they appeared in the First Chakra chapter (see page 52).

Begin by finding a quiet place where you won't be disturbed for about ten or fifteen minutes. Turn off your cell phone or better yet, leave it outside. Make yourself comfortable either in a chair or lying down. It is best if you are sitting to find a chair which supports your spine in an upright position. (It facilitates the movement of the energy.) You may want to cover yourself with a light blanket or throw. Turn the lights down or off. You want to create a comfortable, quiet space where you are not likely to be disturbed.

Close your eyes and take a deep breath. Breathe in as deeply as you can, inhaling through the nose and exhaling through the mouth. Do this for four or five breaths and then begin to exhale through the nose. Continue to think about your breathing, in and out through the nose, until you start to feel yourself relax. To deepen your sense of relaxation, concentrate on your feet. Notice if they feel achy or tense. With your next inhalation, imagine you are sending a feeling of softness and warmth all the way down to your feet and toes. Send your breath to your feet several times if you wish.

Then, when you are ready, with the next inhale, imagine you are sending the breath down to your lower legs, feeling them being covered with warm softness. Feel the tension in your calves let go, and sense them becoming softer and less rigid. Bring that warmth up into your thighs, feeling those powerful quads and hamstring muscles let go and relax. Again, when you are ready, allow that soft, caressing warmth to move up into your lower torso, both front and back, as you feel the tension leaving your lower abdomen, your buttocks, and lower back.

Take a moment to really enjoy the feelings of warmth and relaxation. Then feel the warmth spread further up your body to the chest and the mid-back, loosening any tightness that you find there. Focus again for a moment on your breathing as your chest relaxes more and your breathing becomes easier and deeper. Now bring the soft warmth all the way up your torso, all the way to your shoulders. After a moment or two, check back on your body. It should feel much more relaxed than when you started. If you notice a place or two that still feels tense, send your next outbreath to that (or those) spots. When you feel that you have reached a good state of relaxation, begin to imagine the warmth moving up your neck, both front and back, loosening those neck muscles which often hold a great deal of tension. You may want to take some extra time here if you find a lot of muscle tension. Allow the warmth now to move up the back of your head, covering your entire skull. I often imagine this feeling like a baby's bonnet. Let the warmth then begin to travel down your forehead, smoothing and soothing it. The warmth can then move further down your face, all the way to the jawline.

Now as you are feeling very relaxed, begin by asking your Queen to appear to you in your mind's eye. Since we are in the second chakra, you may see her as a happy, sexy, fulfilled monarch, full of life and love, connected to others, and pregnant with her own self-recognized creativity.

You may see her wearing a beautiful orange robe, as orange is the color of this chakra. At her feet are symbols of the gifts she brings from the second chakra: The Lovers card from the tarot deck, a musical instrument, and an artist's palette to symbolize creativity, and fragrant oils for sensuality. This is your meditation, so feel free to imagine the Queen in the way that most reflects who you are. Her crown might be a garland of meadow flowers or roses. You may see her as heavy with child, glowing with the vitality of new life being created. Her face holds an expression of satisfaction, acknowledging her enjoyment of pleasure with no shame.

Take time to embellish your vision of her adding whatever details seem to belong. As you do this, your second-chakra Queen will become more alive to you.

Now as you continue to hold your vision of her, see her beckon to you. See yourself walking towards her as she gently takes your hand. Ask her to bless you with her creative presence, and to give you all the qualities she represents. See her putting her hand on your head and feel the strength of her energy enter you. Take a moment with this, letting yourself really *feel* it. Let that second chakra energy of the Queen move down from the crown of your head, flow through your whole body all the way down to your feet.

See your Queen happily connected with the important people in her life. Take a minute or two to let this happen. When the visualization feels complete allow the image to fade as you thank your Queen for her blessings and support.

As you continue with your deep breathing, feel yourself returning to your everyday awareness and when you are ready, open your eyes, rub the palms of your hands and the soles of your feet together to bring yourself fully back into your physical reality. When you feel fully back in your body, you may return to your daily activities, knowing that you have done something wonderful and healing for yourself.

Summary
The Queen in the Second Chakra

Below is a short list of the ways in which you can remind yourself of how the second chakra looks in a woman who embodies the Queen.

The Queen:

- Allows her creative juices to flow, knowing they are her gifts and that it is appropriate to explore them, expand them, and share them with others.
- Feels at ease with her body and enjoys the pleasures her senses bring.
- Enjoys the connections, both physical and emotional, that bring her closer to others.
- Works at eradicating past traumas and hurts that have affected her as a sexual being.
- Is passionate about whatever she holds dear, be it people, causes, or her beliefs.
- Is connected to others, her family, her intimates.
- Allows herself to be vulnerable. She is willing to open herself up enough to connect with those she trusts.
- Has the capacity for discernment. She values herself enough not to be preyed upon.

CHAPTER 5

THE QUEEN'S THIRD CHAKRA:
HER SOURCE OF SELFHOOD
AND PERSONAL POWER

The third chakra is located in the area of the solar plexus, on the front and the back of the body. Neuroscience views this area as the second brain, or gut brain, because it is filled with so many neurons and nerve clusters. In Sanskrit, it is known as the *manipura*, a term that is derived from the words *mani*, meaning "brilliant," and *pura*, meaning "house." Tibetan Buddhists refer to it as the jeweled lotus. This energy center relates to ease and comfort with personal power, the ability to use personal power judiciously. It regulates beliefs and opinions, judgment, confidence, and self-discipline, and in the workplace, mastery of your skills and contribution. It is the natural home of the Queen archetype because it deals with power—both power *over* and power *with*. Power *over* and power *with* are directly correlated to the dominator and partnership paradigms discussed in Chapter 2.

The negative side of the third chakra is a constellation of thoughts, feelings, and behavior patterns that are rooted in the misuse, lack of use, or abuse of personal power and the intellect. On the underactive or stagnant side of this constellation is passivity and dependency. On the overactive side is aggression, bullying, and anger.

A woman with a healthy third chakra will manifest self-esteem, a sense of worthiness, self-discipline, and personal agency within her world. As a good Queen would, she values herself highly, and, therefore, can value others equally well. Because she sees herself as innately worthy of all good things, she easily grasps that others have the same right to value themselves. She does not feel diminished by helping others when needed, nor does she see herself only in the role of the helper. Even if she has had to fight a few battles in the past to achieve her sense of personal position, having found herself at home in the seat of power, she feels at ease and able to take and hold the reins when needed.

Confidence and Self-Esteem

Having confidence and self-esteem is easy when we have a strong solar plexus chakra, and cultivating these qualities strengthens this chakra. Often as women we are warned away from cultivating personal agency and from claiming and enjoying power. Since historically women for so long were relegated to supporting roles, we have a cultural hangover. Almost every woman has been discouraged from being personally powerful under certain conditions—perhaps in her home or a primary relationship, perhaps in her workplace. Even today, when a woman exhibits healthy self-esteem, she is often perceived as threatening or warned not to "diminish" the people around her. But things change. Contemporary women are making strides into areas where we have not been before. Therefore, it has become increasingly important to develop confidence and self-esteem. It is also imperative for grown women to help younger women and girls develop self-assurance as well.

Beliefs, Opinions, and Judgment

Our beliefs, opinions, and judgments are products of our sense of our personal power. If we feel unworthy—meaning that we do not believe we are in our rightful places—this sense of being characteristically lacking will be reflected in the types of opinions we hold, the judgments we make, and how we believe things should or do work. But if we have given away our power, our beliefs and opinions will not be strongly held and our judgment will become clouded.

Janet, at fifty-three, was given a promotion that she had worked hard to get. She had "understudied" her predecessor for six months and thoroughly understood what was expected of her. She knew the drill. However, Janet had also thought of a new and better way to handle a portion of her new assignment. She had thought long and hard about how her way would cut the time requirements in half and lessen the chances for mistakes to occur. When she took over the job and began to implement her new ways of doing this part of it, she was severely criticized by her boss and told many reasons why it would not work. She listened respectfully to what her supervisor said and was able to rebut each item, but as the criticism continued she became unsure of her position and rather quickly folded her attempt to stand up for her innovations and finally agreed that she would go back to doing it the tried and true way.

If Janet had had the strength that a healthily functioning third chakra would have provided, she would have been able to more strongly present and defend her ideas and would not have backed down so easily.

Self-Discipline

Self-discipline is a quality we don't seem to hear much about in this century. It seems to have been left behind with archaic ideas like sleeping on hard beds and taking long, cold showers. However, it is a valuable attribute to have. Imagine a self-indulgent queen, sitting on cushy throne, eating bonbons, and taking long naps. It isn't a picture of a powerful monarch, is it? A disciplined Queen, by contrast, would know what needs to be done and when it needs to be done, and be well on her way to seeing that it is done, no matter how she feels about doing it now. In other words, it is duty before pleasure.

In my opinion, one of the best examples of a self-disciplined woman is Queen Elizabeth II. Although she does not rule in the way her predecessors once did when it was a monarchy, she still discharges her many duties of state faithfully, setting aside her personal desires in favor of doing her duty to her country.

Well, you and I are not Queen of England (or likely any other country or principality for that matter). In our less elevated and less complicated lives, we know that we won't be successful in meeting our goals if we do not use our will and determination to "Get up, suit up, and show up."

Boundaries

A Queen needs to have healthy boundaries. Psychologically speaking, boundaries are the awareness and understanding of "where you end and I begin." Boundaries can be material, physical, mental, emotional, and sexual.

Material boundaries include policies like whether you are willing to lend personal items, including money, and to whom, in what set of circumstances.

Physical boundaries are such things as your willingness to hug or give a handshake to someone, how much you value your personal privacy, about the measure of your personal modesty, and whether you feel okay about having closed, locked doors in your home.

Mental boundaries include your thoughts, values, and opinions and whether you can hold on to your beliefs and opinions in the face of another's disagreement with them.

Emotional boundaries have to do with your level of clarity about your responsibility for someone else's feelings and emotions. Having good emotional boundaries keeps you from giving advice or accepting blame. They protect you from feeling guilty for someone else's negative feelings or problems and taking others' comments personally.

Sexual boundaries relate to your comfort level with sexual touch and activity—they are the answers to the questions of what, where, when, and with whom?

Lack of adequate boundaries is the hallmark of many types of crippling dysfunctions, from codependence to borderline personality disorder. Just as a good Queen would assiduously guard the borders of her realm, every woman needs to establish and maintain her own personal borders.

How would these qualities look like in a woman's life—and in your life? Let's consider the story of Maggie.

Raised in a traditionally Catholic home, Maggie heard the nuns at her elementary school talk about being "handmaidens of the Lord." They often acted in a meek and deferential way to the priests of the parish and never asserted themselves in any way to those they saw as being above them in status. Maggie's mother, who was from the old-school mold of deferential women as well, often referred to Maggie's father as the boss or the head of the household. Maggie's parents taught Maggie at an early age that she wasn't equal to anyone else, including even her younger brothers. But Maggie had an innate sense of her own rightness—her right to have her own opinions, her right to act according to her own judgment, a sense of her own personal value.

Even as a Maiden, her sense of being "one unto herself" was prominent. As a woman, she had a strong Amazon orientation—she was a fighter. That early sense of herself seemed to foretell her likelihood of becoming a Queen—or perhaps the highly successful CEO of a large corporation.

Naturally, because of her inner guidance system, Maggie got into all kinds of trouble at school and at home. When she was chastised for following her own instincts rather than obediently doing whatever they said, adults often would call her "headstrong." She was punished sometimes if she wouldn't back down when she felt she was in the right. Later, as an adolescent, with all the pressures of the outside world bearing down on her, she sometimes doubted her feelings and tried to fit in by taking a back seat to others. But as she neared adulthood, she became clearer that her earlier feelings of being secure in her own opinions and power were right for her.

Maggie went on to fight many battles in her life. In the early 1970s, she entered law school. This was a time when it was not easy for women to do this. After passing the bar, she accepted an entry-level position at a prestigious law firm. She worked hard and moved up the ladder. Her Amazon energy and her strong third chakra helped her prepare for and present many cases and win many decisions. But still she had to fight within her firm to get the "good" cases. Her continued hard work and self-confidence brought her the success she sought and now 40 years later as she prepares for retirement, Maggie looks forward to helping and mentoring young women entering the law.

Most of us find it a challenge to reach the level of authentic personal power that Maggie found in herself so readily and relied upon throughout her entire life. Fittingly, the archetype for the third chakra is the Amazon. This type of energy is essential to overcome the obstacles to being self-directed, such as self-doubt, fear of failure, lack of clear boundaries, and lack of tenacity, which is another form of self-discipline.

Personal Power and Self-Direction

Often self-direction is accessed by continuing to listen to our own inner guidance, by paying attention to the insistent nagging thoughts that say, "This isn't working" and then taking action to change it. Sometimes it isn't a simple journey from point A to point B. The story of Arlene illustrates this well.

Arlene is an woman in her fifties who embodies many of the qualities of the third chakra Queen archetype. Arlene had a master's degree in counseling psychology and was on the path to licensure, accruing the 3,000 hours of supervised clinical experience required before being eligible to take her professional boards. Her life took an unexpected turn when she agreed to marry a man she had known well for many years. Marrying George meant moving to Atlanta and starting a new life there.

Initially, Arlene believed she would be finish her licensing requirements in Atlanta and continue down the same career path. As she adjusted to her new life, however, she found it wasn't working in the way she had hoped. She also noticed imbalances, like not being able to spend enough time with friends. Arlene, who had often said, "If I don't enjoy it, I don't do it," found herself feeling like a martyr, which was not a role she had ever found comfortable. To course correct, she shifted her ambitions away from counseling. She studied yoga, becoming a yoga teacher for a while. Then Arlene's marriage ended. It was not everything she had hoped it would be, so after six years, she and George parted amicably. She really found her calling after starting a nonprofit agency to benefit the poor in the Haiti. It was such a powerful experience, that she describes it as a "spiritual awakening."

Arlene spent three years doing charitable work. One of her approaches to helping the poor lead better their lives was to teach them to grow their own food. Unfortunately, her efforts were not successful. Many of the poor, because of their long history of poverty and neglect, seemed to have developed a kind of learned helplessness and had no interest in raising their own food. They preferred to wait for the rations distributed by the government than to participate in farming themselves.

What Arlene realized that inspired her was that even if the impoverished people in the Haiti weren't interested, others might find farming skills valuable. She flew home. Back in Atlanta, she began looking for ways to turn her dream of community food sourcing into a reality. Her adult children pledged to support her. One offered to have her mother live with her so she could save money while her business was in its startup phase and the others offered to help her supplement her income while she got her first project going.

Despite her agenda to feed the poor, as an administrator Arlene had never done any hands-on farming herself up to this point. When an experienced farmer was unable to fulfill his assignment at the community garden, Arlene stepped in, immersing herself in a crash course in urban farming. She loved it and discovered she had a green thumb! While completing this assignment, she met her future farming partners and agreed to join their efforts to create a holistic farming space, located several miles east of Atlanta, dedicated to raising organic, non-GMO produce, available on three weekly market days per week, to local buyers.

As a woman living within the Queen archetype, Arlene has traveled many paths to arrive at exactly the right place she feels she is meant to be. She feels that her destiny is to make a meaningful contribution to the health and wellbeing of the local population wherever she lives. At last report, having applied for and received a grant, she is now expanding her efforts to include teaching grade-school kids how to grow and market healthy, pesticide-free crops.

The Disempowered Queen vs. the Empowered Queen

A deficiency of energy flowing into the third chakra might show up as having a weak will, low physical or mental energy, lack of self-discipline, being easily manipulated by others, having a victim mentality, needing to be right, and being stubborn. The tension you would feel on a physical level can lead to problems with digestion and blood pressure. If you overeat or drink too much in an effort to overcome the disappointment of letting yourself down repeatedly, you could get sick.

The opposite of the third chakra Amazonian-style Queen archetype is the Servant archetype. Finding yourself in the position of being a servant to someone may indicate the need to do further work on your third chakra. But it may not. It depends on the state of your ego. Some people do service out of humility and a desire to give.

Others because they feel inferior. Early in life it may be appropriate to be in a servant state, perhaps while you learn how something is done by assisting a more accomplished individual, but if at midlife or later you find yourself still operating in "assistant mode" this might indicate a need to assess whose ideas are running the show. Putting yourself in a secondary role, may be a way of not claiming your own power. Being a Servant has some payoffs most of us would not want to admit to: if it is carried to an extreme, living off the power and energy of another and never developing your own is a form of power vampirism. It is essential to cultivate your own life force if you are to develop the attributes of the Queen. You need to check in with yourself to determine the motivation behind your own service when it is offered.

A weak third chakra also shows up in relationships. Within couples, it is necessary for there to be equality to have a healthy relationship. This does not mean that partners must be equal in strength in each aspect of their relationship, but it does mean that partners need to be equally important overall in the relationship. Successful couples often have complementary qualities—one makes up for what for the other lacks.

Christina, now in her sixties, carries a great deal of Queen energy. She remarried after more than a decade of widowhood and it is a good marriage; her first was not as happy.

During Christina's first marriage to an older man, she often acceded to her husband's wishes, even when they were in direct conflict with her own. She did not feel she could (or should) stand up to him and insist on things that were important to her, so she did not make an issue of it. Or worse yet, she was often deceptive and devious and thereby managed to get her own way. In her late forties, several years into her marriage, she was diagnosed with depression, began taking antidepressants, and entered therapy for the first time. The psychic pain of the depression fueled her resolve to benefit from this experience and she began to take some hard looks at how she had so often given away her power not only to her husband but also to many others.

As she continued with her therapy and medication, Christina began to reclaim her personal power. After a year she was able to discontinue the meds, because the depression had lifted, but she stayed in therapy, working on many issues, and the focus of the treatment became recognizing her own needs, evaluating, and respecting them, and then finally finding the way to give them at least as much respect as she gave the needs of others. She stopped betraying herself by always giving in.

As a widow, Christina's continued work on power issues and her third chakra became stronger. She attracted a man who appreciated her strength and ability to present her needs and have them met, as she met his. They eventually married—a partnership of a Queen to a King.

Putting Ourselves First

Putting our needs first is often difficult for women, who commonly have spent much of their lives taking care of others. Midlife and the effects of menopause, which occurs during this stage of life, demand that we pay more attention to our own needs. Our changing bodies call for our attention and we may have health-related issues for the first time that we can't ignore. Menopausal weight gain usually gets our attention first. Then the stress of perimenopause and hormonal fluctuations often cause us to reevaluate how we cope and look for answers from less traditional resources. Seeking answers from both traditional and alternative medicine may introduce us to new regimens to help us find a new place of balance.

Often, midlife with its new challenges and opportunities will initiate growth and prompt us to seek psychological and spiritual support through psychotherapy or spiritual inquiry. Honor yourself for asking for assistance when you do. This is a time when putting yourself first is necessary to help you restructure the foundation of your life for the rest of your life.

Meeting the Queen in Your Third Chakra

As you did when exploring the previous chakras, if you would like to meet the Queen in your third chakra, invite the Queen to come through you as you go about your daily activities. Also write in your Queen's journal and meditate upon who she is for you. Take all the time you need or want to experiment with your journaling and meditation about the Queen's third chakra aspects, before moving on to the next chapter.

Inviting the Queen to Come Through You

Because you are now focused on your third chakra, you may want to spend some time thinking about how the Queen would express herself as a powerful, self-directed being. She may do this by setting clear and strong personal boundaries with others, by taking responsibility for her own life, and by taking control of her fate. She will respect her own personal beliefs and opinions, freely express her personal identity and enjoy her self-assurance. She will act with discipline and exercise clear judgment. She will treasure her mental abilities, cultivating them and using them well. She will make the best decisions she possibly can for herself and others, when appropriate. Most of all, she will be her own woman. If you are not doing or feeling all these things yourself yet, by reflecting on them you are building the potential in you for this archetype to manifest. A personal vision will come into focus.

As you engage in creative visualization about the Queen archetype, breathe into the area of your third chakra (both on the back and front of your body at the level of the solar plexus) and invite her to enter your body. Try being the Queen as you attend a networking luncheon, your book club, or a professional conference. Notice how that changes your experience of what you are doing. Does it enrich the experience? And do you enjoy yourself more? Does it seem to affect your interactions with others? Do you like how you feel?

You might find it interesting to imagine what it would be like if you were the one in charge of a particular gathering where you are not the leader or the host. How would you do it differently? This is not meant as an exercise in usurping another's power, but in introducing you to the idea of what it might be like for you to take a leadership position in your own life, if you haven't already.

Again, remember the qualities that are held in the third chakra: power over yourself, appropriate use of power over others when in a leadership role, good boundaries, independence, and good use of your mental abilities.

Journaling About the Queen

You will need paper and a pen to complete this exercise. Or you can park yourself in front of your laptop. Just be sure you are comfortably seated and somewhere you won't be interrupted.

As you did for the first chakra journaling exercise (see page 52), begin by thinking of any situation in your life where third chakra qualities (power, judgment, opinion, intellect, inner direction, motivation) are problematic for you. When you find an issue that you would like to focus on, take some time to imagine several ways you might possibly solve or resolve this problem.

An example: You have wanted to ask for a promotion to a managerial job which you know you would do well. Your concern is that you would have trouble supervising others and telling them what to do, particularly since you would be promoted above your present coworkers and would have to assume a "power" position over them. How would you be able to do that? Would your leadership be adequate? How would you resist any attempts from them to dismiss your leadership because they "knew you when"?

Now, ask the Queen to show herself to your mind's eye. What do see first about her? Flesh her out. See her in detail. What is she wearing? Perhaps somewhere in her clothing you will find a touch of golden yellow. (Yellow is the color associated with this chakra.) What does her crown look like? Mentally ask her to help you clarify the image. Feel yourself expanding and growing, still seeing your problem, although from a higher perspective. Hold this perspective for as long as you can, asking the Queen to help you see the issue.

Then go back to looking at your situation and review it as the Queen. Embody her. If you are following the instructions written above, your sense of rightful power will begin to shift toward the sure recognition that you have always known that you have the gift of leadership, because you are a Queen, and power is your right. You will see that you have earned the right to leadership and as the Queen you have the skill to lead others. Can you imagine a Queen feeling like she has no right to lead? Or feeling apologetic for her abilities to help others reach their highest level of performance?

It is with this new awareness of who you are becoming that you open the door to this archetypal energy and the possibilities for the resolution of your issues.

Let's say another situation you have chosen to work on is your lack of confidence in your own sense of right direction. It seems like a good idea, but you have reservations about it. Spend some time really thinking again about the problem and your solution. Look at it from different aspects, seeing if it might not be a hangover from the bad old days of chronic self-doubt. See if your concerns about your resolution aren't an opportunity to rethink the problem and come up with a better answer. Try and imagine the Queen being undone by having to reconsider how to address a problem. She wouldn't be undone, just thankful that she is following her own inner knowing and looking for a better answer.

I suggest that when you experience self-doubt, you don't treat it as a flaw; rather, if you know yourself to be intuitive, view it as a possible intuitive warning. You can use intuitive hunches to guide you beyond logic.

When you feel you have clarity on the third chakra issue, open your eyes and write in your journal. Describe everything you saw, heard, felt, and understood. Write in a stream of consciousness without censorship. Let the Queen speak on the page if she wants to. Let this be a sacred, regal experience of beautiful self-connection. An act of self-love.

Third Chakra Meditation

Another powerful way to invite the Queen into your third chakra is in meditation. Many women enjoy using this type of meditation to start or end their days.

For your convenience, I am repeating the following relaxation induction instructions as they appeared in the earlier chakra chapters. Begin by finding a quiet place where you won't be disturbed for about ten or fifteen minutes. Turn off your cell phone or better yet, leave it outside. Make yourself comfortable either in a chair or lying down. It is best if you are sitting to find a chair which supports your spine in an upright position. (It facilitates the movement of the energy.) You may want to cover yourself with a light blanket or throw. Turn the lights down or off. You want to create a comfortable, quiet space where you are not likely to be disturbed.

Close your eyes and take a deep breath. Breathe in as deeply as you can, inhaling through the nose and exhaling through the mouth. Do this for four or five breaths and then begin to exhale through the nose. Continue to think about your breathing, in and out through the nose, until you start to feel yourself relax. To deepen your sense of relaxation, concentrate on your feet. Notice if they feel achy or tense.

With your next inhalation, imagine you are sending a feeling of softness and warmth all the way down to your feet and toes. Send your breath to your feet several times if you wish.

Then, when you are ready, with the next inhale, imagine you are sending the breath down to your lower legs, feeling them being covered with warm softness. Feel the tension in your calves let go, and sense them becoming softer and less rigid. Bring that warmth up into your thighs, feeling those powerful quads and hamstring muscles let go and relax. Again, when you are ready, allow that soft, caressing warmth to move up into your lower torso, both front and back, as you feel the tension leaving your lower abdomen, your buttocks, and lower back.

Take a moment to really enjoy the feelings of warmth and relaxation. Then feel the warmth spread further up your body to the chest and the mid-back, loosening any tightness that you find there. Focus again for a moment on your breathing as your chest relaxes more and your breathing becomes easier and deeper. Now bring the soft warmth all the way up your torso, all the way to your shoulders. After a moment or two, check back on your body. It should feel much more relaxed than when you started. If you notice a place or two that still feels tense, send your next outbreath to that (or those) spots. When you feel that you have reached a good state of relaxation, begin to imagine the warmth moving up your neck, both front and back, loosening those neck muscles which often hold a great deal of tension. You may want to take some extra time here if you find a lot of muscle tension. Allow the warmth now to move up the back of your head, covering your entire skull. I often imagine this feeling like a baby's bonnet. Let the warmth then begin to travel down your forehead, smoothing and soothing it. The warmth can then move further down your face, all the way to the jawline.

Now as you are feeling very relaxed, begin by asking your Queen to appear to you in your mind's eye. Since we are in the third chakra, you may see her as a powerful, self-directed monarch, full of strength and mental clarity, a guardian for those under her protection and leadership, with self-confidence in her own abilities.

You may see her wearing a beautiful golden yellow robe, as yellow is the color of this chakra. Her crown might be a made of solid gold and encrusted with precious jewels. At her feet are symbols of the gifts she brings from the third chakra: The Empress from the tarot deck is a good representation of her: a scepter and orb, which are symbols of a worldly queen's power; balancing scales, signifying her ability to find the balancing point in any situation; a sword to represent her warrior-like nature.

This is your meditation, so feel free to imagine the Queen in the way that most reflects who you are. Take time to embellish your vision of her adding whatever details seem to belong. As you do this, your third chakra Queen will become more alive to you.

Now as you continue to hold your vision of her, see her beckon to you. See yourself walking toward her as she gently takes your hand. Ask her to bless you with her powerful presence, and to give you all the qualities she represents. See her putting her hand on your head and feel the strength of her energy enter you. Take a moment with this, letting yourself really *feel* it. Let that third chakra energy of the Queen move down from the crown of your head, flow through your whole body, all the way down to your feet.

See your Queen leading people in her life with a sureness of purpose. Take a minute or two to let this happen. When the visualization feels complete allow the image to fade as you thank your Queen for her blessings and support.

As you continue with your deep breathing, feel yourself returning to your everyday awareness and when you are ready, open your eyes, rub the palms of your hands and the soles of your feet together to bring yourself fully back into your physical reality. When you feel fully back in your body, you may return to your daily activities, knowing that you have done something wonderful and healing for yourself.

Summary
The Queen in the Third Chakra

Below is a short list of the ways in which you can remind yourself of how the third chakra looks in a woman who embodies the Queen.

The Queen:

- Feels comfortable in taking the reins of power because she knows how to lead.
- Recognizes and cherishes her mental abilities.
- Feels in control of herself and is able to decide a course of action and follow through.
- Knows where her power ends and another's begins.
- Respects her own and others' physical and emotional boundaries.
- Respects her own instincts and intuition and follows them.
- Does not depend on others' validations of her plans and actions.

CHAPTER 6

THE QUEEN'S FOURTH CHAKRA: HER SOURCE OF UNENDING LOVE AND COMPASSION

The fourth chakra is known as the heart chakra, or *anahata*, a Sanskrit word that means "unstruck," "unbeaten," or "unwounded" and refers to the beating of the heart which makes a sound without percussion. The heart is an instrument that beats with compassion and emanates the silent, yet perceptible sound of love. In the physical body, the heart chakra supports and regulates the heart, the lungs, the circulatory system, the thymus gland, the immune system, the upper back, the skin, and the hands.

The health of the fourth chakra builds on the successful development of the energy of the first three chakras. The fourth chakra is love, and you cannot be open to love unless you are well grounded in your survival (first chakra), able to feel desire (second chakra), and respectful of your own power and that of others (third chakra). For a woman to embody the Queen fully, she needs to be able to love with an open heart while respecting her own vulnerability. This is not a matter of fear but of enlightened self-protection. We all have our vulnerabilities and an internal sense of what is safe for us and what is not. We may be feeling generous with our love and affection and at times feel almost giddy with the joy of sharing our love. We wouldn't compromise our physical safety by offering our love and affection to those who may not treat it as a gift, but as a way to exploit us. Also, we would not offer our love to someone we already know would not treat our love with the respect it deserves In other words, we have already learned that those "dangerous men" who once seemed desirable, are not worthy of our love.

The heart chakra may be seen as a bridge. Being the center chakra of the seven principal chakras, it bridges the lower, more physical chakras with the three higher, more spiritually oriented chakras. Also considered a bridge between the material, human realm (the Earth) and the immaterial, spiritual realm (heaven), this energy center helps us to integrate wisdom and insights. It helps us to connect with others in a strong way, regulates our relationships to others and ourselves, and facilitates transformation.

The negative side of the fourth chakra is a constellation of unhealthy thoughts, feelings, and behavior patterns that are rooted in the areas of giving and receiving, self-acceptance, forgiveness, and having broken heart.

Love at the Queen Level

What does the Queen's love look like in this fourth chakra? It is both more personal and yet less personal than the love she has demonstrated in the past. At this stage of life, you know who you are, so you no longer look to love for definition. Earlier in life you may have used love to help you see more clearly who you are. The love your beautiful baby showed you enhanced your belief in your ability to be the loving mother you wanted to be. Likewise, your lovers or partners helped you feel more the loving, desiring, and desirable woman you wanted to see yourself as. Those characteristics have been internalized and integrated into your psyche—and if they have not, you have some work to do on yourself to love yourself more.

If you are a Queen, you are secure in your ability to love and be lovable. You know you possess qualities that can attract and hold the interest of a partner and lovers and that you are capable of loving them back. Because we cannot love fully unless we love ourselves, let's assume you have a healthy dose of self-love and have spent a good deal of your adult life loving and caring for others in some capacity to reach the moment where your heart is open to love freely. As the archetypal energy of the Queen combines with your personal energy, you will feel assured of love's presence in your life. Many women feel wounded by their experiences with love. They feel as if they have given themselves away to someone and did not get the love they hungered for in return. They have lost the ability to trust themselves to feel love—especially romantic love. So, they are stingy with their love, and count and measure how much love they get— and what kind—against their expectations. This is a road to disappointment.

For Claudia, a divorced woman of fifty-five, love had often seemed to her to be a commodity of sorts; something to be measured out when given and something to be carefully weighed when received. Like most of us, Claudia had had her heart broken more than once, beginning in early childhood. Her mother, whom she adored, had been stingy with the love she showed Claudia, fearing to overwhelm the three-year-old Claudia with how much she really loved her only child. Claudia had had no way of knowing her mother was intentionally, for her own reasons, not showing love to her and only perceived it as her basic unworthiness to receive *all* of her mother's love. Add to that the heartbreaks she had felt from disappointments she had experienced in her marriage and other love relationships, and you can see how fifty-something Claudia saw love as something to be measured both when it was given to her and when she loved back. With each of the people in her life whom she loved, she did not let the love just flow through, but instead carefully assessed how much she felt she was getting and then returned only what she saw as an equal amount. The first fallacy here is that love cannot be adequately measured, either coming in or going out. So, the outcome in these situations was not based on any real measurement of love, but on a defensive posture meant to spare Claudia of any more heartbreak. The result was that Claudia never felt adequately loved and her heart was never allowed the joy of just loving—the very essence of heart's work.

As a Queen, your heart chakra empowers you to love in balance—just to let it flow without needing to measure how much goes out against what is seen to come back in. The Queen can see love flowing within her realm and she is happy to contribute to it, but she knows her existence does not depend upon it.

Let's look at Jeanne's story. Jeanne, age sixty-two, has a strong, enduring love for her husband, Tom. They have been together for thirty-five years and are successful parents of two children and doting grandparents. Their marriage has undergone all the predictable stresses and troubles of most marriages. There was even a time when they considered divorce due to Tom's overwork and increasing dependence on alcohol. The close call of separation gave them the chance to reassess their situation and their commitments to each other and their family and they decided that staying together would be worth all the work it would entail. Now with longed-for retirement on the horizon, Tom's health is seriously challenged. He has been diagnosed with colon cancer and has begun chemo and radiation. Although she would miss her husband, Jeanne has been imagining herself alone again. *What would it be like?* she wonders.

Jeanne, influenced by the archetypal energy of the Queen, sees possibilities for her future in a way that is different from the way a woman still under the influence of the Mother archetype. With all her heart, she wants Tom to be able to beat the cancer and to continue the journey of their lives together. At the same time, she realizes that this may not be possible. As a younger woman still under the influence of the Mother archetype, she might not have been as able to simultaneously hold two opposing possibilities in mind and make plans for either eventuality. With her Queen's vision, she can foresee what might lie ahead and is able to consider strategies and prepare herself for possible widowhood.

Jeanne's responses are at once complex and simple. She recognizes the possible outcomes of this major event in her life, and despite her sense of grief at the possible loss, is able, like a good executive, to consider options and make plans for both herself and her husband. What would be the best care for Tom? How can she make sure he has everything that can be provided for him? How can she support his emotional needs as well as her own? These are questions emanating from the loving heart of a Queen. As a competent, mature woman, she can hold the tension of the opposites, by planning for eventualities while still loving and fighting fiercely for her husband's return to health.

The Disempowered Queen vs. the Empowered Queen

As we all know, it takes courage and fortitude to love fully. As was touched upon earlier, opening our hearts to love can put us at risk for disappointment, hurt, and rejection. The Empowered Queen is secure enough in herself to knowingly take those risks, after having decided that they are worth taking and that she is not putting herself in unnecessary jeopardy. Having reached a stage in life where she has been hurt by love before, she knows the pain and knows that she can endure it if she must.

By contrast, the Disempowered Queen only plays at love, giving the impression to herself and others that she has opened her heart fully. But the truth is she is acting a part and never fully gives of herself. It's as if she has an escape route already in place so when it feels to her that she is about to face any of love's disappointments she is ready to exit stage left. It's easier than one would imagine, but that is because she never fully committed. She thereby loses what love could have brought her, because she was only playing at love.

Compassion and Empathy

Compassion has many synonyms, as among them *concern, benevolence*, and *kindheartedness*, all of which describe emotions or feelings found on the "love spectrum" that emanate from the heart chakra. We may feel benevolent toward a person or a concept.

The word *compassion* seems to carry with its meaning a sense of less personal involvement, of some slight removal from its object--as in feeling compassion for the victims of the hurricane. Empathy, on the other hand, describes the experience of feeling, in our bodies, the sensations of what we imagine another person is feeling as if her feelings were our own. Highly empathetic people can pick up what others are feeling at the time they are feeling it because of this sensitivity.

As a woman embodying the Queen archetype, your ability to feel both compassion and empathy are greatly enhanced by your life history. On your way to becoming a Queen you undoubtedly felt pain on many occasions. No one goes through life without experiencing losses and tragedies. These have "tenderized" you, like someone cooking barbecue would soften a tough piece of steak. Most likely, by now you can well imagine what another is feeling in her present state. You have lived long enough to recognize their pain for what it is and your heart responds by embracing the other in loving oneness. Often this leads us to attempt acts of kindness and charity, anything to relieve the suffering we perceive.

Perhaps Jane's experience will help illuminate the difference between compassion and empathy.

Jane is a sixty-something, long-divorced woman with no

children. Even though she is still working full-time in a telecommunications firm, for many years she has volunteered with a nonprofit agency to make and deliver bagged lunches to the homeless. She feels a connection with the homeless, because as a child she never felt sure of the stability of her own home. Her mother often moved her small family of three daughters, due to the difficulties for a single mother working and raising a family alone in the bygone era of the 1950s. In the Fifties, it was extremely difficult for women to earn enough money to raise a family. You could be a nurse, a teacher, a secretary, or work in retail. That was about it. It may have been a boom time for some Americans, but not for single mothers. Money was always tight, sometimes the rent did not get paid on time, and the family lived under a constant threat of eviction.

As a little girl, Jane was very afraid she wouldn't have a home to go home to. As a successful adult, she found comfort in thinking that her work and the work of the non-profit she volunteered for might help some other child feel less afraid. Jane's compassion for the homeless was rooted in her personal experience.

One Saturday, while delivering lunches at a homeless encampment, she saw a little girl crying inconsolably. She brought a lunch to her and asked what was making her cry. Through her sobs, the girl said that her pet dog, Dolly, had been hit by a car that morning and died. Jane's heart lurched in her chest and tears sprung to her eyes as she felt the grief that child was feeling. She had not lost a pet as a child, so this was not rooted in an actual memory, but her heart knew and felt another's pain because she was able to keep her heart open as she listened.

Meeting the Queen in Your Fourth Chakra

As you did when exploring the previous chakras, if you would like to meet the Queen in your fourth chakra, you may invite the Queen to come through you as you go about your daily activities. Also write in your Queen's journal and meditate upon who she is for you. Who are you when you embody her? Take all the time you need or want to experiment with your journaling and meditation about the Queen's fourth chakra aspects, before moving on to the next chapter.

Inviting the Queen to Come Through You

Because you are now focused on your fourth chakra, you may want to spend some time thinking about how the Queen would express herself as a loving, compassionate being. She may do this by adopting an abundant approach to giving love. She no longer counts the amount of love given and does not measure the love received. She sees it as a never-ending supply and knows her inflow and outgo will never be exhausted. She sees love as an element that exists outside herself and herself as a conduit through which it flows

As you engage in creative visualization about the Queen archetype, breathe into the area of your fourth chakra (both on the back and front of your body at the level of the heart) and invite her to enter your body. Try imagining what it would feel like to spend a day or a week being a vessel of love. See yourself filling up with love and do your best to go through a day, minute by minute, expressing love. Beam universal love at the grocery store, at the dry cleaners, when you are with your family or friends, or even better (because it is so challenging to do so), while driving on the freeway. How does this change your perception of the day, and of the people to whom you sent love, including yourself? To play off a frequently used phrase: *Try being the love you are longing for.*

Journaling About the Queen

You will need paper and a pen to complete this exercise. Or you can park yourself in front of your laptop. Just be sure you are comfortably seated and somewhere you won't be interrupted.

As you did for the first chakra journaling exercise (see page 52), begin by thinking of any situation in your life where fourth chakra qualities (for example, love, compassion, empathy, affection) are problematic for you. When you find an issue that you would like to focus on, take some time to imagine several ways you might possibly solve or resolve this problem.

An example: Let's say you find that you have trouble feeling compassionate toward people suffering from drug addiction. After all, haven't they brought this on themselves? Nobody forced them to begin using drugs or continuing to use drugs while their lives fell apart. Perhaps you have never used illegal drugs because you know better—in fact, you have always believed that drug use brings nothing but personal and physical ruin, so you never tried it. Instead of compassion for addicts, you feel a little smug and self-righteous.

Having defined the issue, take some time to acquaint yourself with the many reasons people use and become addicted to substances. Then think of the reasons that someone might have gotten hooked without the intention to do so. The opioid crisis is a good example. Trusting medical patients were given pain medications to overcome chronic pain or to get through the pain associated with a medical procedure. Some of these medications have strongly addicting properties and when the prescriptions run out there are no more to be had. At this point, many people have already reached a level of physical dependence and need these drugs just to function. Without the help of a recovery program, their lives soon become chaotic as they spiral down a predictable path of addiction.

After trying to imagine what it feels like to be in someone else's situation, you may realize that the smug, judgmental indifference you feel is your own attempt to distance yourself from her pain. It is judgment that constricts your heart and doesn't allow it to feel compassion. This makes for a small heart, one that is bound up and defended.

When you embody the Queen, you are at a higher level than that. You know you can see pain, and the person behind the pain, and to greet such a one with love.

Now, ask the Queen to show herself to your mind's eye. What do see first about her? Flesh her out. See her in detail. What is she wearing? Perhaps somewhere in her clothing you will find a touch of clear emerald green or pink or both. (Green and pink are colors often associated with this chakra.) What does her crown look like? Is it gold with precious jewels? You may even see her as the Queen of hearts in a card deck! Mentally ask her to help you clarify the image.

Now, feel yourself expanding and growing stronger, still seeing your problem, although from a higher perspective. Hold this perspective for as long as you can, asking the Queen to help you see the issue clearly.

Then go back to looking at your situation and review it as the Queen. Embody her. If you are following the instructions written above, your sense of loving will begin to shift, helping you realize how strong your heart is. Strength and love have been intertwined forever.

A Queen's heart is strong. She is courageous enough to face and overcome any challenge. In 1588, during the war of the English against the Spanish armada, Queen Elizabeth I of England gave a famous speech to rally her troops to fight for victory in which she made this point well. She said: "I know I have the body of a weak and feeble woman; but I have the heart and stomach of a king, and a king of England too. . . ." (You will need to overlook the sexist tone of her quote and realize it was a product of her time.)

The root word for courage is *cor,* Latin for "heart." Having embraced the Queen archetype you realize that you have acknowledged your own strength to love is there because you have had the heart and the courage to love even the most difficult people.

When you feel you have clarity on the fourth chakra issue, open your eyes and write in your journal. Describe everything you saw, heard, felt, and understood. Write in a stream of consciousness without censorship. Let the Queen speak on the page if she wants to. Let this be a sacred, regal experience of beautiful self-connection. An act of self-love.

Fourth Chakra Meditation

Another powerful way to invite the Queen into your fourth chakra is in meditation. Many women enjoy using this type of meditation to start or end their days.

For your convenience, I am repeating the following relaxation induction instructions as they appeared in the earlier chakra chapters.

Begin by finding a quiet place where you won't be disturbed for ten to fifteen minutes. Turn off your cell phone or better yet, leave it outside. Make yourself comfortable either in a chair or lying down. It is best if you are sitting to find a chair that supports your spine in an upright position. (It facilitates the movement of the energy.) You may want to cover yourself with a light blanket or throw. Turn the lights down or off. You want to create a comfortable, quiet space where you are not likely to be disturbed.

Close your eyes and take a deep breath. Breathe in as deeply as you can, inhaling through the nose and exhaling through the mouth. Do this for four or five breaths and then begin to exhale through the nose. Continue to think about your breathing, in and out through the nose, until you start to feel yourself relax. To deepen your sense of relaxation, concentrate on your feet. Notice if they feel achy or tense. With your next inhalation, imagine you are sending a feeling of softness and warmth all the way down to your feet and toes. Send your breath to your feet several times if you wish.

Then, when you are ready, with the next inhale, imagine you are sending the breath down to your lower legs, feeling them being covered with warm softness. Feel the tension in your calves let go, and sense them becoming softer and less rigid. Bring that warmth up into your thighs, feeling those powerful quads and hamstring muscles let go and relax. Again, when you are ready, allow that soft, caressing warmth to move up into your lower torso, both front and back, as you feel the tension leaving your lower abdomen, your buttocks, and lower back.

Take a moment to really enjoy the feelings of warmth and relaxation. Then feel the warmth spread further up your body to the chest and the mid-back, loosening any tightness that you find there. Focus again for a moment on your breathing as your chest relaxes more and your breathing becomes easier and deeper. Now bring the soft warmth all the way up your torso, all the way to your shoulders. After a moment or two, check back on your body. It should feel much more relaxed than when you started. If you notice a place or two that still feels tense, send your next outbreath to that (or those) spots. When you feel that you have reached a good state of relaxation, begin to imagine the warmth moving up your neck, both front and back, loosening those neck muscles which often hold a great deal of tension. You may want to take some extra time here if you find a lot of muscle tension. Allow the warmth now to move up the back of your head, covering your entire skull. I often imagine this feeling like a baby's bonnet. Let the warmth then begin to travel down your forehead, smoothing and soothing it. The warmth can then move further down your face, all the way to the jawline.

Now as you are feeling very relaxed, begin by asking your Queen to appear to you in your mind's eye. Since we are in the fourth chakra, you may see her as strong, loving monarch, full of compassion and empathy, an unending supply of love for those in her orbit, with a sureness of self-love.

You may see her wearing a beautiful, emerald-green robe trimmed with pink, as both these colors are associated with *anahata*. Her crown would certainly be solid gold, as nothing is as precious as love. It may be jeweled with jade, rose quartz, green tourmaline, and green calcite as these are the crystals and gems associated with the heart chakra. Scents from essential oils that evoke this chakra are rose and ylang ylang. At her feet are symbols of the gifts she brings from the fourth chakra, such as a heart symbolizing love and a lion symbolizing her courage.

The Queen of Cups from the tarot deck is a good representation of the Queen archetype in the fourth chakra. The card shows the Queen of Cups sitting on her throne with water lapping around her feet, symbolizing emotion. Her cup is covered, symbolizing a containment of emotion. Also, hers is the only decorated cup in the deck, symbolizing the higher level of love represented here—a selfless love.

This is your meditation, so feel free to imagine the Queen in the way that most reflects who you are. Take time to embellish your vision of her adding whatever details seem to belong. As you do this, your fourth chakra Queen will become more alive to you.

Now as you continue to hold your vision of her, see her beckon to you. See yourself walking toward her as she gently takes your hand. Ask her to bless you with her powerful presence, and to give you all the qualities she represents. See her putting her hand on your head and feel the strength of her energy enter you. Take a moment with this, letting yourself really *feel* it. Let that fourth chakra energy of the Queen move down from the crown of your head, flow through your whole body all the way down to your feet.

See your Queen with love flowing to all around her, holding her love with courage and constancy. Take a minute or two to let this happen. When the visualization feels complete allow the image to fade as you thank your Queen for her blessings and support.

As you continue with your deep breathing, feel yourself returning to your everyday awareness and when you are ready, open your eyes, rub the palms of your hands and the soles of your feet together to bring yourself fully back into your physical reality. When you feel fully back in your body, you may return to your daily activities, knowing that you have done something wonderful and healing for yourself.

Summary
The Queen in the Fourth Chakra

Below is a short list of the ways in which you can remind yourself of how the fourth chakra looks in a woman who embodies the Queen.

The Queen:

- Does not measure the love she gives and receives—but lets it flow.
- Is not defined by the love she gives and received—She already knows who she is.
- She can hold the tension of the opposites. She can feel pain, grief, even despair, while still able to strategize how to overcome or live with the obstacles.
- She can love bravely and freely, without fearing the pain that the loss of a love would bring, because she has already felt mortally wounded in love and has survived and she knows that she will continue to survive and love.

CHAPTER 7

THE QUEEN'S FIFTH CHAKRA: HER CENTER OF COMMUNICATION AND SELF-EXPRESSION

The fifth chakra is located in the area of the throat, a physical region that incorporates everything between the shoulders and the ears: ears, mouth, teeth, tongue, palate, vocal cords, thyroid, parathyroid, and jaw. In Sanskrit, this energy center is known as *vishuddha*, a word that means "purification." It regulates verbal and nonverbal communication and creative expression, especially the act of projecting your ideas and visions into the world. This would include doing things like writing a book, building a house from a blueprint of your own design, exhibiting your paintings in a gallery, and so on. Fifth chakra energy is intimately related to the refinement of your purpose. It also is strongly connected to the second chakra, where creativity begins; the difference is that now this creative energy is being projected outwardly into the world.

The fifth chakra physically regulates the health and function of a wide range of physical senses and organ systems: hearing and speaking, and sound modulation; dental health and jaw function, which are associated with digestion and food consumption; the tongue and the sense of taste; and the thyroid and parathyroid glands, and their associated hormones, which help to regulate our metabolic processes.

The negative side of the fifth chakra is a constellation of thoughts, feelings, and behavioral patterns related to holding back the expression of your deepest truth. For instance, if you are experiencing a creative urge and not acting on it or allowing it to grow so you may share it with your community and the world, you may find that your energy is becoming blocked and you are experiencing symptoms in your throat.

Clear and Articulate Speech and Open Listening

A woman with a healthy fifth chakra will be able to talk about her emotions, thoughts, and opinions openly, freely, and with confidence. She allows herself to be vulnerable and authentic in conversation. She can control her speech, not feeling that she must interrupt when others express different views or speak over people to get her point across. She can listen to what they are saying without feeling her own opinions are being diminished. She enjoys sharing her creative endeavors and delights in the reception of her gifts without becoming inflated.

A healthy throat chakra helps a Queen express herself clearly, so that she may easily use nuanced language to allow listeners to grasp the intricacies of her thoughts. Her speech will be creative and imaginative and rarely banal and vapid. There is richness to her style of communication, but also a directness. She offers enough detail to flesh out the meaning of what she is saying, so she will be understood, but not so much as to overwhelm her listener.

A well-functioning throat chakra allows the Queen equally good listening skills. She listens attentively, waiting to formulate her response when a speaker has finished speaking rather than not really listening because she is trying to devise what she will say next. She is respectful of what people say and can discern falseness and subterfuge.

Controlled Speech

The Queen is able to control her speech. Having reached a position of authority in her own life, she no longer feels a need to yell to get her point across. Recently, there has been a disruption in basic civility and it is most obvious in the media. It seems to show up most prominently in cable news programs. Typically, there is a panel of pundits discussing some newsworthy incident. Assumedly, each of them has some level of knowledge of and expertise in the subject presented, but instead of allowing one another to speak with some semblance of structure, the conversation soon devolves into a melee of mutual interruption, which usually ends with raised voices and participants talking (or screaming) over each other. Nothing is heard, but the winner seems to be the one who has most aggressively dominated. The Queen can hold her own place in such conversations and not be talked over or down to.

However, repressed speech should not be mistaken for controlled speech, which is when a woman fails to express herself in order to maintain a façade of harmony in a situation. The Queen is never a people pleaser.

A good example of how this works is Joan's story. As an example, Joan, aged fifty-seven, is the mother of two and the grandmother of five. She and her husband, Ron, aged fifty-nine, who is the father of her adult children, live together and consider themselves close. Not anymore, but for many years, Joan followed her introverted personality and her natural desire for harmony by seldom speaking up for what she wanted or believed was right. As she entered her fifties, she noticed feelings of discomfort in her throat and neck area. There was so much tension in her neck muscles that her dentist diagnosed her with TMJ syndrome after she complained of jaw pain and tooth wear that indicated some teeth grinding. Joan suffered from sore throats and hoarseness, as she had all her life, believing that her throat was her weak spot. When hyperthyroidism in the form of Graves' disease showed up, she knew there was something going on in her throat.

Joan had been doing kundalini yoga, a type of yoga that focuses on the energy body, for the preceding two years and had been working diligently with her chakra system. She wondered if what she was seeing was an imbalance in her fifth chakra and an indicator of a need for some inner work. As a Queen, she always took painstaking care of her health. Joan knew to systematically work on the psychological issues that she felt might be the cause of weakness in this area. By looking deeply into how she communicated, the quality of both her speaking and her listening, she became aware of how much more she needed to value what she had to say, and also how she needed to actively hear others.

Joan asked her husband to support her in this and they discussed how their own dynamic worked. Ron began to see how they had each played into an unconscious exchange in which Joan often repressed her feelings and opinions so that she could "agree" with him and uphold their mutual desire to appear perfectly compatible, to have a united front. Joan saw that in her own mind she was still cherishing an outmoded model of the "good wife."

Joan and Ron's adult children did not at first seem to be aware of any change in Joan, but slowly began to see how she spoke up more and began to listen more attentively to them. Over time, Joan became a more influential presence in her family's life and her input was increasingly valued.

Joan noticed bit by bit that there had been another series of changes: her TMJ pain and the bruxism (the technical word for teeth-grinding) had stopped, her neck muscles weren't so tight, and she only rarely had sore throats. The greater energy and improved balance in her fifth chakra was both the indicator and the strengthener of her ability to communicate at the level expected of a woman under the influence of the Queen archetype.

Sharing Your Creative Endeavors

A creation of any kind needs to be shared to fulfill its reason for being. A painting that spends years in a closet, unseen and unappreciated, brings little to the world or its creator beyond the pleasure of the initial act of creation. The manuscript, meant to become a published book, read and appreciated by others, which instead lives in file cabinet, unfinished and unread, has not fulfilled its creator's original intention. In the Judeo-Christian tradition, it is put forth that God created humans to share the joys and appreciation of His creation.

A woman who has psychologically matured to the level of the Queen customarily will want to share her creative abilities and works of art with others, believing that what she offers is valuable and will be of benefit to them. She is self-confident enough not to let any timidity or shyness keep her from adding her gifts and visions to the world.

The story of Louise gives us an example of how this might show up. As a young child of four or five, Louise heard her mother say things that gave Louise the impression that artists were very special people given a gift at birth of "being artistic," so only a few of us have that gift and she wasn't one of them. Louise grew up believing anything she did that was artistic was doomed to fail because she didn't have the right gift.

There were several years of trying different career paths after graduating college. Louise finally realized how much she wanted to become an interior designer. She had worked as an editorial assistant at a regional interior design publication and become aware that she might have some talent for design and enjoy doing it professionally. She loved color and setting up inviting, comfortable spaces. Louise looked into the accredited design programs at local colleges and universities and found a program that seemed to fit her needs and her pocketbook, and enrolled for the fall quarter. In a phone conversation with her mother, when she announced her plans enthusiastically, the response she got was, "Who ever told you that you are an artist?"

Louise was momentarily blindsided by her mother's response, but immediately recalled her mother's view that being artistic was only available to very special people. She felt the familiar hurt of the remark and quickly shook it off, realizing she should have expected it. Much loss and harm had been caused by accepting this belief in the past. In this recognition, Louise was freed to go beyond her mother's limited belief because she found it of no benefit. She carried on. Louise had become her own authority about the value of her gifts and was able to follow her plan, even if her mother didn't believe in it.

Disempowered Queen vs. the Empowered Queen

It is relatively easy to affect the throat chakra because its front side is located so close to the surface of the body; it has little covering to protect it from picking up thoughts, feelings, and negativity from others. Even though the chakra penetrates the body, extending from the front of the throat to the back of the neck, this is a slender part of the body. There is little protection, such as muscle, ribcage, or body mass.

Many women have found that even if they can embody the qualities of the Queen associated with most of, or all the other chakras, when looking at the throat chakra's workings there is some surprise. A woman may feel deeply rooted to the earth, her home, and her family. She may be comfortable with her sexuality and adept at the proper use of power. She may know deeply that she loves and receives love, but when it comes to expressing her creativity or clearly speaking her truth, she falters or gives in to shyness or modesty.

Some of this dysfunction or reservation may come from childhood experiences in which a woman was not allowed to speak freely, or from later in childhood when expressing her views brought derision or dismissal from others. Her lack of ability to express herself may also come from the patriarchy's old-fashioned cultural view that women should not speak up. Or cultural views that speaking up is "bragging" and therefore wrong. The disempowered Queen will be unable to express her feelings articulately, and she may also find herself drawn to lesser forms of communication, such as idle gossip, complaints, and such. Meaningless chatter and harmful gossip are injurious to the throat chakra. They drain the center's energy and leave a speaker feeling unheard and unseen authentically.

The empowered Queen will be able to bridge the heart's emotional energies of love and compassion with the more mental energy qualities of the sixth chakra, which we shall discuss in the next chapter. She will be able to clearly realize what it is that she needs to say. She will be able to distill and clarify her thoughts, and then say what she needs to impart with simplicity and passion.

Signs Your Fifth Chakra May Be Out of Balance

The throat chakra can become unbalanced because of the chakra not receiving adequate energy or because of introversion, timidity, shyness, and insecurity. However, an overactive throat chakra may also contribute to gossiping, nonstop talking, and being verbally aggressive by shouting, talking over others, and frequently interrupting people. When you have an overactive fifth chakra, it may seem as though the conduit between the thoughts you have in your mind and what comes out of your mouth is not working--or is missing entirely, making it impossible to get out your thoughts.

Other symptoms of an unbalanced throat chakra are having a "little" or insignificant voice that is hard to hear or making a habit of speaking tentatively. Also, if you find that you often lie, this would indicate the need to balance the fifth chakra. Not being able to keep secrets and being highly secretive also are indications of an imbalanced fifth chakra.

For the Queen, it is very important to have the fifth chakra functioning at an optimal level, because not only does the Queen need to be able to communicate effectively, she also must be clear in her intentions about how she communicates. Communication begins with telling your own truth. Lying and deception weaken the throat chakra and are not compatible with embodying the Queen.

To reach the level of Queenhood, a woman must have developed authenticity and believe in what she says. To say it in a more down to earth way, it is being a "straight shooter"—not necessarily saying everything bluntly and without grace but being able to communicate that what you are saying is true, so it hits the mark. Can you imagine holding Queen energy in your own life and NOT speaking the truth?

Effective, well-considered, and kind communication is another hallmark of a Queen. The Queen shares herself primarily by communication. Her speech and her attentive listening nearly define who she is. With her thoughtful speech, she conveys the truth as she understands it and can imbue that speech with meaning and complexity. She knows how to win others over to her perspective by knowing HOW to speak to them. By having listened attentively to their stories, her intuition guides her to speak back to others in a way they will most easily take it in. In the lives of real-life queens this capacity is known as statecraft or diplomacy, and in its everyday expression it is just as effective for us as it is for those monarchs.

Meeting the Queen in Your Fifth Chakra

As you did when exploring the previous chakras, if you would like to meet the Queen in your fifth chakra, you may invite the Queen to come through you as you go about your daily activities. Also write in your Queen's journal and meditate upon who she is for you. Who are you when you embody her? Take all the time you need or want to experiment with your journaling and meditation about the Queen's fifth chakra aspects, before moving on to the next chapter.

Inviting the Queen to Come Through You

Because you are now focused on your fifth chakra, you may want to spend some time thinking about how the Queen would express herself with clarity. She may do this by giving thought to everything she expresses, making sure she is saying what she really means in the clearest, most compassionate way she can. She sees her truth as being worthy of being heard, because she sees herself as a woman of value and substance. She sees self-expression as the completion of her every creative endeavor—to her, if she creates it but does not put it out into the world, her effort will be incomplete and the value of her creativity severely diminished.

As you engage in creative visualization about the Queen archetype, breathe into the area of your fifth chakra (both on the back and front of your neck) and invite her to enter your body. Try imagining what it would feel like to spend a day or a week being the voice of creation. See yourself filling up with a verbal expression of creativity and go through a day, minute by minute, seeing how you might express this in words.

Also visualize yourself saying exactly the right thing in the best way as you interact with others at work, with your family and friends, or with strangers you encounter as you go through your day. How might saying the right thing in the best way impact your day or the people with whom you spoke, or how you feel about yourself.

Journaling About the Queen

You will need paper and a pen to complete this exercise. Or you can park yourself in front of your laptop. Just be sure you are comfortably seated and somewhere you won't be interrupted.

As you did for the first chakra journaling exercise (see page 52), begin by thinking of any situation in your life where fifth chakra qualities (for example, clarity of speech and displaying your artistic gifts) are problematic for you. When you find an issue that you'd like to focus on, take some time to imagine several ways you might possibly solve or resolve the problem.

An example: you might find that you have trouble speaking up about your position on a controversial subject. The conversation is already launched and someone else is speaking strongly against your so far undeclared position. After having expressed his or her opinion in no uncertain terms, this person passes the conversational ball to you, expecting that you will agree and add further credence to his or her position. You feel on the spot, but there is no way your integrity will allow you to mumble something that might sound like agreement and pass it off. On the other hand, you do not want to go *mano a mano* on this subject. How do you honor your own position and your well-thought-out opinions without making an enemy?

As the woman embodying the Queen archetype, you might want to summon all the compassion and gravitas you can and respond with measured words and tone, stating your position in a way that does not leave the other feeling like he or she must defend his or her beliefs. I am aware that this isn't always an easy thing to do, but when you withhold any indication that there is a contest between you, you help other people recognize that you are willing to see opposite positions stand side by side without the need for a "winner."

Now, ask the Queen to show herself to your mind's eye. What do see first about her? Flesh her out. See her in detail. What is she wearing? Perhaps somewhere in her clothing you will see a beautiful light aqua, reminding you of the sea on a gentle, sunny day. This is the color associated with this chakra.

What does her crown look like? Perhaps in this visualization she is wearing a light and airy tiara made of silver, with stones that sparkle like sunlight bouncing off gentle ocean waves as they wash the shore. Mentally, ask the Queen to help you clarify her image. Feel yourself expanding and growing stronger, still seeing your problem, although from a higher perspective. Hold this perspective for as long as you can, asking the Queen to help you see it clearly and in detail.

Then go back to looking at your situation and review it as the Queen. Embody her. If you are following the instructions written above, you will begin to feel your focus changing and becoming clearer, helping you realize how easily your mind and heart can align. Once the mind and heart are aligned the words you intend to write in your journal will come easily.

When you feel you have clarity on the fifth chakra issue, open your eyes and write in your journal. Describe everything you saw, heard, felt, and understood. Write in a stream of consciousness without censorship. Let the Queen speak on the page if she wants to. Let this activity reflect a marriage of right perspective and loving self-acceptance.

Fifth Chakra Meditation

Another powerful way to invite the Queen into your fifth chakra is through meditation. Many women enjoy using meditation to start or end their days.

For your convenience, I am repeating the following relaxation induction instructions as they appeared in the earlier chakra chapters.

Begin by finding a quiet place where you won't be disturbed for about ten or fifteen minutes. Turn off your cell phone or better yet, leave it outside. Make yourself comfortable either in a chair or lying down. It is best if you are sitting to find a chair that supports your spine in an upright position. (This facilitates the movement of the energy.) You may want to cover yourself with a light blanket or throw. Turn the lights down or off. You want to create a comfortable, quiet space where you are not likely to be disturbed.

Close your eyes and take a deep breath. Breathe in as deeply as you can, inhaling through the nose and exhaling through the mouth. Do this for four or five breaths and then begin to exhale through the nose. Continue to think about your breathing, in and out through the nose, until you start to feel yourself relax. To deepen your sense of relaxation, concentrate on your feet. Notice if they feel achy or tense. With your next inhalation, imagine you are sending a feeling of softness and warmth all the way down to your feet and toes. Send your breath to your feet several times if you wish.

Then, when you are ready, with the next inhalation, imagine you are sending the breath down to your lower legs, feeling them being covered with a warm sensation. Feel the tension in your calves let go, and sense them becoming softer and less rigid. Bring that warmth up into your thighs, feeling those powerful quads and hamstring muscles let go and relax. Again, when you are ready, allow that soft, caressing warmth to move up into your lower torso, both front and back, as you feel the tension leaving your lower abdomen, your buttocks, and lower back.

Take a moment to really enjoy the feelings of warmth and relaxation. Then feel the warmth spread further up your body to the chest and the mid-back, loosening any tightness that you find there. Focus again for a moment on your breathing as your chest relaxes more and your breathing becomes easier and deeper. Now bring the soft warmth all the way up your torso, all the way to your shoulders.

After a moment or two, check back on your body. It should feel much more relaxed than when you started. If you notice a place or two that still feels tense, send your next outbreath to that (or those) spots.

When you feel that you have reached a good state of relaxation, begin to imagine the warmth moving up your neck, both front and back, loosening those neck muscles, which often hold a great deal of tension. You may want to take some extra time here if you find a lot of tension.

Allow the warmth now to move up the back of your head, covering your entire skull. I often imagine this feeling like a baby's bonnet. Let the warmth then begin to travel down your forehead, smoothing and soothing it. The warmth can then move further down your face, all the way to the jawline.

Now, as you are feeling very relaxed, ask the Queen to appear to you in your mind's eye. Since we are in the fifth chakra, you may see her as a powerful spokesperson, fully aware of the complexity of the issues at hand and secure in her position and in the best way to express her convictions without insisting it is the only position to hold.

You may see her wearing a beautiful aqua-colored robe, the color associated with *vishuddha*. Her crown would be sparkling silver. At her feet would be symbols of the gifts she brings from the fifth chakra, such as the completion of the act of creation, which is some form of expression. You might see this as the infinity symbol—a figure eight on its side—showing that you cannot have half the loop without the other half, as you cannot have creativity without expression.

This is your meditation, so feel free to imagine the Queen in the way that most reflects who you are. Take time to embellish your vision of her, adding whatever details seem to belong. As you do this, your fifth chakra Queen will become more alive to you.

Now, as you continue to hold your vision of her, see her beckon to you. See yourself walking toward her as she gently takes your hand. Ask her to bless you with her powerful presence, and to give you all the qualities she represents. See her putting her hand on your throat and feel the strength of her energy enter you. Take a moment with this, letting yourself really *feel* it. Let that fifth chakra energy of the Queen move down and flow through your whole body all the way down to your feet.

See your Queen with integrity and clarity emanating from her.

Take a minute or two to let this happen. When the visualization feels complete, allow the image to fade as you thank your Queen for her blessings and support.

As you continue with your deep breathing, feel yourself returning to your everyday awareness and when you are ready, open your eyes and rub the palms of your hands and the soles of your feet together to bring yourself fully back into physical reality. When you feel fully present in your body, you may return to your daily activities, knowing that you have done something wonderful and healing for yourself.

Summary
The Queen in the Fifth Chakra

Below is a short list of the ways in which you can remind yourself of how the fifth chakra looks in a woman who embodies the Queen.

The Queen:

- Sees her own inner wisdom and is willing to share it with others.
- Is not afraid to risk confrontation or dissent from others when she speaks her truth.
- Values other's thoughts and opinions, even when they are different than her own.
- Learns how to say things in a way that reaches others and which they can accept and act upon.

CHAPTER 8

THE QUEEN'S SIXTH CHAKRA: HER CENTER OF INTUITION

The sixth chakra is located between the eyebrows. In Sanskrit it is known as the *ajna* which means "command" and "perception," and is a highly important control center of the body. It is here that we are able to use our conscious control for our own wellbeing. It is here that we decide and mobilize what will most benefit our physical mental and spiritual wellbeing. It is here where we can use the combination of left and right brain functions: our left-brain functions of analysis and logic with our right brain qualities of vision, intuition, imagination and wisdom. This energy center is where the personal "I" meets the universal cosmos; where we perceive subtle energy movement and sometimes find illumination. It is said the *ajna* is controlled by the pineal gland located deep in the center of the brain and that calcification of the pineal caused by harmful heavy metals impedes the function of this gland and hence the third eye chakra. If you are interested in knowing more about decalcifying the pineal gland there are several online sites which describe this process. The sixth chakra governs our intellect and insight gives us access to unseen internal worlds and supports our connection with the spiritual world.

According to Ambika Wauters in her book, *Chakras and Their Archetypes: Uniting Energy Awareness and Spiritual Growth,* "It is also the seat of psychic and artistic gifts and where the heights of our imagination can inspire us."

The third eye chakra also affects the health of the eyes and the brain. It is important to remember that the chakra system is not in the physical body but is part of the subtle or energy body often referred to as the "soul" or "spirit." There is much esoteric information on awakening or opening the third eye, but it is not the intention of this book to address that. That work is best undertaken with a skilled and trusted spiritual teacher.

The negative side of the sixth chakra is a constellation of thoughts feelings and behavior patterns that are rooted in fantasy or lack of clarity or imagination. Rigidity in thought and action and mental confusion may signify a less than optimally functioning third eye chakra. When this chakra is blocked you can start to distrust your inner voice and can lean toward a more negative vision of your life and your future. Clinging to the past and fear of the future can lead you to holding on to dogmatic beliefs and adhering to a very rigid daily routine. A lack of sixth chakra energy can result in the complete dismissal of the validity of all that is not purely physical and scientifically provable.

Vision and Wisdom

A woman with the sixth chakra qualities of vision and wisdom will value her abilities to see the bigger picture noting how she and her life are in exactly the right place at the right time. She has seen this over and over again when her personal (ego-centered) will has sent up the alarm that this or that has to happen right now she has looked back and realized that the longed-for event did finally occur at the perfect time a time she was not able to foresee earlier. As a woman with the ability to see or imagine the best possible outcome she is confident that the event (or another even better one) will come into play when it is time. This woman has the patience and the faith to hold her vision of the outcome. The woman embodying the Queen archetype in the sixth chakra senses the movement of subtle forces which shape her world, and this adds to the complexity of her vision.

Intuition Psychic Ability and Spiritual Connection

The online site Dictionary.com defines intuition as a direct perception of truth, fact, etc. independent of any reasoning process; an immediate apprehension. It is a word or concept which is often spoken of and often misunderstood. It is sometimes referred to as an "Aha moment" when everything comes together with clarity. Intuition is a "knowing" when despite there not having been careful analysis or logical reasoning you just know that something is true or right. It exists in us all along with our higher reasoning abilities. It is not magical or paranormal nor it is well understood. Since you are reading this book and have stayed with it thus far I think it is safe to assume that you have had experience with intuition. So rather than trying to explain the unexplainable, let's look at how your use of your intuition can enhance your decision-making abilities and add immeasurably to your life as a woman living in the Queen archetype.

Leslie had always prided herself on her "common sense" and agile mind. She had always gotten good grades in school because she realized early on that she "had a good mind" and took personal pride in her clarity of thought and grasp of details. She was at ease with her mental acuity finding it usually easy to make decisions by looking at the facts sorting the pros from the cons and arriving at a plan of action that she expected would work. In all her fifty-seven years in her small successful business as a bookkeeper, she had relied on her abilities to see "just the facts" and arrive at a good decision. This time it was different. She had met someone.

Leslie had spent most of her adult life as a single woman. Some of that was, she believed, her choice. She had wanted her business to succeed and had put her heart, soul and time into that goal besides which she had never met anyone before who had captured her heart. But this was different. The man she had just met and to whom she had a powerful attraction was not the type of man she had envisioned for herself. There was something about him that seemed wild and free and just a little bit dangerous. He had asked her to have dinner with him this week and she had asked him if she could get back to him the next day.

Instead of spending Wednesday closing her client's books at the end of the current quarter, as she needed to do to stay on schedule, she spent several hours at a local library looking at books of poetry. She was looking for a poem which might help her see more clearly what she was feeling. Leslie puzzled at her new behavior: she had not read poetry in a long time and had not felt this way in a much longer time. She did find her poem and she felt herself resonate with its message. She felt a door had been opened but she didn't know where the passage it revealed would take her. Her trusty pals, common sense and a good mind, weren't being of much help in indicating whether she should move towards the open door.

Leslie remembered having recently come across an article online about using intuition to help with difficult decisions. She located the article and reread it. It gave her some idea of how she might evoke her own intuition on this matter and she wasted no time in implementing it. Leslie still new to the idea of her own intuition, spent some time alone engaging her feelings rather than just facts. To be sure this was a very new way for her to approach a question, but she felt sure that she got a go ahead to accept his invitation. It turned out to be a lovely evening, one which helped her see herself a little differently as a woman who could learn to listen to an inner voice and find its value.

Finding Your Intuition

It may help if you become even more aware of your strengths in working with your intuition. If you have ever taken the Myers-Briggs test and gotten the result which is always four letters such as INFJ, ESTP, ENTJ, ISFP, etc. you may remember your result. If you have never taken the test, another similar test, is available to the public under the name Keirsey Temperament Sorter. You can find it online at www.keirsey.com.

I would suggest you take the test and have them score it online. Your result will either have the letter N or S in the second position.

The N indicates Intuition and S stands for Sensate. These two words indicate the primary way you receive information from your surroundings. If you are sensate you will receive most of your information through your five senses. You will be a clear observer of details will most likely have keen senses of smell and taste as well as hearing sounds distinctly. If you have an N it will indicate that you get information through your intuition where there is less clarity of detail and sensory input. Intuitive awareness is more like seeing the breadth and texture of an entire landscape with little awareness of its individual components. In other words, you see the lawn but not the individual blades of grass. With intuition you see more patterns and fewer details and I believe it is this awareness of patterns which helps us more completely understand that there is a larger context for everything.

If you find you are a sensate type, do not despair—this doesn't mean you are lacking in intuition. We all have it. For you, as intuition is not your primary function, you may have to be a little more patient to access it. The first information you perceive generally will be from your physical senses. Don't discount those, of course. Your primary mode of perception is most valuable. Continue to engage with the issue at hand, however, and look for information that does not originate from your five senses but has a sense of knowing to it. This will be your intuition.

You may want to explore more about the Temperament Sorter and I urge to do so it is a fascinating study of personal typology which can help you better understand yourself as well as other people and their innate differences and strengths.

I also believe that the Third Eye is a contributor to psychic insight. The *ajna* chakra is a portal for external life energy (also called *prana* or *chi*) to enter and be allocated to the other chakras. It is also a key to ongoing spiritual development. Thus, keeping it as clear and balanced as possible is very important.

Imagination and Wisdom

Sixth-chakra imagination and wisdom are universal and transcendent in nature. The sixth chakra when highly developed elevates consciousness and confers deep spiritual insight and awareness. Perception of non-ordinary reality may accompany this.

Imagination is one of the attributes that separates humankind from the other animal species and is a spark of the divine light which is our birthright. As we continue to evolve under the Queen archetype we may see that our imagination becomes stronger. As babies we came in with our imagination fully engaged but as we grew up in this world which generally doesn't support that which is unseen our imaginative qualities lessened. By the time we reach the biological age to enter the Queen's realm our abilities to imagine vividly may have taken a hit. For those of us who have been involved with our artistic qualities we may find our imagination is still intact and may even be well developed. But whatever the case we can increase our abilities to imagine in any number of ways primarily by working with the arts in their various forms.

Wisdom stemming from the sixth chakra often presents in that often-experienced sense of knowing. Most likely we have experienced that knowing in one form or another throughout our lives but it is during this time of the influence of the Queen archetype that we may feel it more often and more strongly.

The Third Eye chakra is also said to be the home of the archetypes. It may be that in the imaginal realm of this chakra, the archetypes find their natural home. If so it is another excellent reason for learning more about this chakra and how to keep it clear and open.

How can a Queen use her intuition and farseeing-ness to benefit both herself and those within her realm? Some ways certainly will include becoming more aware of the imaginal world and the imaginative parts of herself. Being more familiar with these secret parts of herself such as her dreams, her awareness of symbols and their meanings are good ways to start. As the Queen develops she may feel drawn to artistic expressions in ways that she had not really considered in the past. Experimenting with painting, drawing, dance, and poetry may now unlock some as yet unrealized richness in her interior life. Many women have not had the time or leisure to attend to their own muses when they were busy bringing up children, running a home or business, and just trying to get from point A to point B. But now with fewer daily demands on her time a woman under the Queen Archetype may find promptings to try forms of expression she has never before considered. As she delves further into her imagination she may find her interior monologue becoming stronger; she may find symbols, colors, and movements which stir her in unanticipated ways.

Penny is a good example of how this can work. The later part of Penny's career was as a city administrator. She loved the work and became adept at using the many skills it called for. She learned how thoughtful planning addressed the many complexities of running a small city government. She understood how to play the political game often necessary to get things done. But she had not found the time before retirement to look inside herself and see what she was ready to express in her own life. The mother of a gifted dancer, Penny, had spent much of her life helping her daughter pursue her dream of artistic excellence, and she took great pride in Jennifer's success. But now it was her turn, too. Penny began by taking a pottery class in an adult education program at a local college. She quickly found that the molding of clay into sensuous shapes and glazing the fired result with any color or sheen she could devise was immensely satisfying. Her newfound hobby quickly moved into being an important element in her life and provided her with a deeper understanding of herself and the world around her. As her interior life grew it added a richness and dimension to every aspect of her life and heightened her self-awareness. As her eyes developed an artistic discernment she realized how the slight shifting of a line here or a different proportion changed how something looked. That knowledge easily translated into a more global awareness for her of how small changes and refinements may make all the difference in things other than pottery. Penny moved from being a retiree to an artist.

The Disempowered Queen vs. the Empowered Queen

The disempowered Queen will disregard any information she encounters unless it is scientifically provable. She does not give credence to immaterial elements in her life. As an example, a disempowered Queen overly wedded to her mental powers of logic, data collecting, statistical proof, rejects the imaginal, mythic, and spiritual truths severely limiting her experience of life. The disempowered Queen by rejecting all nonphysical, scientifically unproven elements of life greatly impoverishes her own awareness. She will also be unable or unwilling to use her intuition to guide or confirm her movement towards a goal. She may distrust her own inner knowing, seeking always to find validation from outside sources.

The empowered Queen will be aware of her own intuition and how it works for her. She will recognize the ways in which her intuition makes its awareness known and will be willing and able to follow that inner knowing. The empowered Queen will treasure her hard-won wisdom, remembering what it took for her to reach this level and will use it in every aspect of her life. The empowered Queen is intimately involved in her own spirituality whether she believes in a personal god or sees her god in nature and in the magnificence of the universe. The empowered Queen also sees her place and value in that universe.

Signs Your Sixth Chakra May Be Out of Balance

Physical symptoms that your Sixth chakra may be out of balance are headaches, vision (eye) problems sinus problems and certain kinds of hormone dysfunction. Emotionally sixth chakra problems may show up as moodiness, rapid mood changes, and an inability to self-reflect.

Intellectually a lack of clarity, an inability to see the big picture, being stuck in the details, the inability to hold a personal vision for yourself and the rejection of everything spiritual and inexplicable are other symptoms of lack of balance in this chakra. Having an overactive third eye chakra can bring a different set of concerns. You may experience fantasies, visions and nightmares that can be truly frightening. Intrusions from the astral plane may threaten your feelings of sanity. This imbalance can also result in distortions of spiritual truths.

However, when this chakra is balanced we feel clearly focused and can see the difference between truth and illusion. We are open to receiving wisdom and insight.

Meeting the Queen in Your Sixth Chakra

As you did when exploring the previous chakras if you would like to meet the Queen in your sixth chakra you may invite the Queen to come through you as you go about your daily activities. Also write in your Queen's journal and meditate upon who she is for you. Who are you when you embody her? Take all the time you need or want to experiment with your journaling and meditation about the Queen's sixth chakra aspects before moving on to the next and final chakra the Crown.

Inviting the Queen to Come Through You

Because you are now focused on your sixth chakra you may want to spend some time thinking about how the Queen would experience herself here. You may do this by assessing your own personal nature (perhaps using the Keirsey Temperament Sorter if you need help to see how your intuition functions; see Resources). If you find that you are more sensate than intuitive, don't see that as a lack but as an opportunity to work more with your intuitive side to enhance its performance. Since this can be done in many different ways, you may want to explore this with a spiritual teacher or an experienced *kundalini* yoga instructor. If you realize as a result of this internal assessment that you are indeed intuitive you may look for new ways to employ intuition in your daily life. You might pay attention to synchronicities that are showing up in your life and begin keeping an informal journal of them on a daily or weekly basis. If you do not have a meditation practice you may consider beginning a daily meditation practice for ten to twenty minutes. (See meditation section below).

Begin to consciously engage your natural imagination. If your life has not given you enough opportunities recently to exercise your imagination, why not do a few things that will reengage the active imaginings of childhood. One excellent source of this is not, unsurprisingly, children. If you have not spent some time recently in the company of kids under seven make an opportunity for yourself to do so. Children have open access to imagination and being in their presence and interacting with them can give a giant boost to your own imagination.

To give you a personal example of this I worked for a few years as a therapist with young children who had emotional difficulties, either seeing them in their homes or at school in a private setting. Most of the therapeutic work was in "play therapy," since the children were too young to engage in "talk therapy." Since the type of play was up to the individual child each one decided on what we would do for that hour. Imagination played the starring role with each child exercising his/her own flights of fancy by telling stories (with some prompting from me) about their doll or the picture they were painting. They were expressing their creative imagination while my imagination was greatly stimulated by accompanying them.

As you engage in creative visualization about the Queen archetype, breathe into the area of your sixth chakra and invite her to enter your body. Try imagining what it would feel like to experience that internal "knowing" in answer to a problem or consideration you are presently experiencing. See yourself thinking about the problem going over all they already examined solutions or options then imagine your sixth chakra Queen helping your intuition and insight magically ramp up giving you clarity and an out-of-box approach.

Journaling About the Queen

You will need paper and a pen to complete this exercise. Or you can park yourself in front of your laptop. Just be sure you are comfortably seated and somewhere you won't be interrupted.

As you did for the first chakra journaling exercise (see page 52) begin by thinking of any situation in your life where you would like to see your sixth chakra qualities (for example insight and wisdom) enhanced. When you find an issue you'd like to focus on, take some time to reacquaint yourself with what you have already deduced.

Now having written down the above question and those already thought of answers ask the Queen to help you find a better solution by expanding the parameters of your thinking. This may not happen immediately. You may need to allow time for new, better answers to appear. You might wait hours, days, or even weeks. The answer might not come in the expected way. Be alert to your dreams: answers often show up here. Also, so-called stray thoughts may show up. Before waving them off like buzzing insect take a curious look to see if your answer is coming to you this way. Review this part of your journal frequently so as to consciously remember each of the things you are working on.

Now ask the Queen to show herself to your mind's eye. What do see first about her? Flesh her out. See her in detail. What is she wearing? Perhaps somewhere in her clothing you will see a beautiful indigo, reminding you of the depth of the darkness on a moonless night. This is the color associated with this chakra.

What does her crown look like? Perhaps in this visualization she is wearing a silver crown with the crescent moon at its center or a five-pointed star, both of which are associated with this chakra. Mentally ask the Queen to help you clarify her image. Feel her presence growing stronger within you and feel a sense of clarity as she makes her presence palpable. Hold this perspective for as long as you can, asking the Queen to help you see it clearly and in detail.

Then go back to looking at your situation and review it as the Queen. Embody her. If you are following the instructions written above, you will begin to feel your focus changing and becoming clearer helping you realize how easily your mind and heart can align. Once the mind and heart are aligned the words you intend to write in your journal will come easily.

When you feel you have clarity on the sixth chakra issue open your eyes and write in your journal. Describe everything you saw, heard, felt, and understood. Write in a stream of consciousness without censorship. Let the Queen speak on the page if she wants to.

Sixth Chakra Meditation

Another powerful way to invite the Queen into your sixth chakra is through meditation. Many women enjoy using meditation to start or end their days.

For your convenience, I am repeating the following relaxation induction instructions as they appeared in the earlier chakra chapters.

Begin by finding a quiet place where you won't be disturbed for about ten or fifteen minutes. Turn off your cell phone or better yet leave it outside. Make yourself comfortable either in a chair or lying down. It is best if you are sitting to find a chair that supports your spine in an upright position. (This facilitates movement of the energy.) You may want to cover yourself with a light blanket or throw. Turn the lights down or off. You want to create a comfortable, quiet space where you are not likely to be disturbed.

Close your eyes and take a deep breath. Breathe in as deeply as you can, inhaling through the nose and exhaling through the mouth. Do this for four or five breaths and then begin to exhale through the nose. Continue to think about your breathing in and out through the nose until you start to feel yourself relax. To deepen your sense of relaxation, concentrate on your feet. Notice if they feel achy or tense. With your next inhalation, imagine you are sending a feeling of softness and warmth all the way down to your feet and toes. Send your breath to your feet several times if you wish.

Then when you are ready with the next inhalation, imagine you are sending the breath down to your lower legs, feeling them being covered with a warm sensation. Feel the tension in your calves let go and sense them becoming softer and less rigid. Bring that warmth up into your thighs, feeling those powerful quads and hamstring muscles let go and relax. Again, when you are ready, allow that soft, caressing warmth to move up into your lower torso, both front and back, as you feel the tension leaving your lower abdomen, your buttocks, and lower back.

Take a moment to really enjoy the feelings of warmth and relaxation. Then feel the warmth spread further up your body to the chest and the mid-back, loosening any tightness that you find there. Focus again for a moment on your breathing as your chest relaxes more and your breathing becomes easier and deeper. Now bring the soft warmth all the way up your torso, all the way to your shoulders.

After a moment or two, check back on your body. It should feel much more relaxed than when you started. If you notice a place or two that still feels tense, send your next outbreath to that (or those) spots.

When you feel that you have reached a good state of relaxation begin to imagine the warmth moving up your neck, both front and back, loosening those neck muscles which often hold a great deal of tension. You may want to take some extra time here if you find a lot of tension.

Allow the warmth now to move up the back of your head, covering your entire skull. I often imagine this feeling like a baby's bonnet. Let the warmth then begin to travel down your forehead, smoothing and soothing it. The warmth can then move further down your face all the way to the jawline.

Now as you are feeling very relaxed, ask the Queen to appear to you in your mind's eye. Since we are in the fifth chakra you may see her as a powerful spokesperson fully aware of the complexity of the issues at hand and secure in her position and in the best way to express her convictions without insisting it is the only position to hold.

You may see her wearing a beautiful indigo colored robe, the color associated with *ajna*. Her crown would be sparkling silver. At her feet would be symbols of the gifts she brings from the sixth chakra such as a crystal ball to signify psychic abilities, a diploma signifying an excellent intellect, a wizard's hat symbolizing wisdom and connection with the unseen.

This is your meditation so feel free to imagine the Queen in the way that most reflects who you are. Take time to embellish your vision of her adding whatever details seem to belong. As you do this your sixth chakra Queen will become more alive to you.

Now as you continue to hold your vision of her see her beckon to you. See yourself walking toward her as she gently takes your hand. Ask her to bless you with her powerful presence and to give you all the qualities she represents. See her putting her hand on your throat and feel the strength of her energy enter you. Take a moment with this letting yourself really *feel* it. Let that sixth chakra energy of the

Queen move down and flow through your whole body all the way down to your feet.

See your Queen with wisdom and mental clarity emanating from her. Take a minute or two to let this happen. When the visualization feels complete allow the image to fade as you thank your Queen for her blessings and support.

As you continue with your deep breathing feel yourself returning to your everyday awareness and when you are ready open your eyes and rub the palms of your hands and the soles of your feet together to bring yourself fully back into physical reality. When you feel fully present in your body you may return to your daily activities knowing that you have done something wonderful and healing for yourself.

Summary
The Queen in the Sixth Chakra

Below is a short list of the ways in which you can remind yourself of how the sixth chakra looks in a woman who embodies the Queen.

The Queen:

- Sees life more clearly and with a broader, wider perspective.
- Sees patterns in all facets of life—the seasons, human history, attitudes and habits in her life and in the lives of those important to her.
- Is aware of the power she holds because she is more aware than before, and she uses that power or ability to help others understand that not everything is rooted in physicality.

CHAPTER 9

THE QUEEN'S SEVENTH CHAKRA: HER CROWN OF SPIRITUAL CONNECTION

Located at the top or "crown" of the head, the seventh chakra links the individual to the universal. In Sanskrit, it is called the *sahasrara,* which means "1,000-petaled lotus." Energetically, it ensures a connection to universal sources of energy, and to the entire world.

Physiologically, the seventh chakra is the body's primary coordination center, as it is associated with the pituitary gland, the brain, and the central nervous system. Imbalances to the seventh chakra may create physical dysfunctions that lead to depression, high blood pressure, and migraines.

On an emotional level, a balanced seventh chakra allows for expanded awareness. It gives you access to your subconscious mind, allowing you to see your true nature and accept yourself as part of the wider universe. This chakra supports and promotes understanding, emotional stability, enlightenment, connectedness to all that is, and awareness of our connection to the Divine. Through forming a deep connection to *sahasrara,* you may fulfill your highest potential as a woman in midlife and beyond.

In earlier centuries, it was believed that kings and queens had a right to rule that came directly from God, that they were emissaries with a mandate from the Supreme Being. Even though this seems inflated by today's standards in terms of social hierarchies, the seventh chakra corresponds to a similar concept of connection to the Divine Source—on an individual basis. The woman living within the Queen archetype has a sense of being on a spiritual mission. Without connection to Divine Source, however that may be understood by her, there would be no queenhood. The Queen is working at a higher level than she was earlier in her life, and her being now resonates with the presence of divine energy or a sense of a higher purpose.

Now, there can be a Queen who does not acknowledge her connection to a divine source and sees her accomplishments as the result of her own doing. Religious sentiment or belief is not essential, *per se,* for achieving the psychological stature of a Queen. But if a woman believes that all that she has done has occurred because of her initiative alone, *without assistance,* and she does not credit anything or anyone outside of herself, then, of course, this will limit her vision of what could be accomplished. If she sees the exclusive source of her good as herself, her accomplishments by definition must then be as limited as her own sense of herself and of her individual talents and skills. There is a lack of depth in this point of view.

The complexities of a woman's vision cannot exceed what she can imagine. The Queen needs to hold space for the grace that might come in and expand her potential. Call this grace an accident, or call it the Divine, or call it the way of nature. It is the sense of having access to resources beyond herself that is significant. Not the name she knows grace by. There is evidence that an attitude of *pronoia,* believing the universe has your back, opens the filters of your perception so you experience more good.

An example of this might be seen in Patricia's story. Patricia had a logical, linear, and scientific way of approaching life's challenges. When her second grandchild was diagnosed with Down's syndrome, she initially viewed it as a tragedy. She read everything she could, learning about the causes of the condition, the expectations for the boy's life, the possible length of his life, and all the difficulties which he might encounter. Having been an atheist all her life, Patricia disregarded the ideas of a divine source and the possibilities that might manifest from unexpected synchronicities and unlooked-for interventions. She looked exclusively to the medical community to provide help for her grandson. Logic and science were her "deities."

Patricia had expected this grandchild would be a healthy, physically perfect child and this perfection would bring the same kind of joy that her first grandchild had brought to her. In her disappointment, she saw her second grandchild's condition as burden for the family.

What Patricia came close to missing was that her grandson, with all the problems that Down's syndrome may bring, was the embodiment of love and brought a level of joy and appreciation for the moment to her that no one and nothing else had. Patricia began to believe that this child had an important contribution to make to the life of their family and to her, by expanding her way of thinking about how things "should be."

By connecting with unconditional love on the level of her seventh chakra, Patricia found she could love and care for her grandson wholeheartedly. With her newly-opened heart and enhanced expectations of what his life could be, she did not feel as driven to fix him or to attempt to determine why he was as he was. She had connected to her own definition of divine source and saw his presence as a gift.

Connection to Spirit

Women who are maturing into the role of the Queen most likely have many dependents. To psychologically, physically, and spiritually balance their own needs against those of the people in their "realms" is no small feat. Their awareness of the necessity to relinquish their egoic idea that they can do everything themselves eventually leads all to search for solutions that enable them to replenish their own reserves. Making a connection to a higher power, including the power of nature or of silence, or even their own better nature, a familiar aspect of their lives, is a discipline they learn to cultivate. They do so by studying the habits of high performers and establishing routines that soothe and replenish their spirits.

When I was asked by my book editor which of the chakras was my "favorite," I had to think about it for a while. They all have their own unique characteristics. After considering the question for a while, I realized that the seventh chakra was my favorite, because it encompassed the concept of grace—that gift of the Divine. What that said to me was that I had another source of help and support and that I could call on that to raise the level of my endeavors higher—that it wasn't all up to me.

There are three long-held spiritual traditions that can help strengthen your connection to the Divine or the sacred part of your being, your higher self or your soul: fasting, meditation, and prayer. Spiritual writings from different world cultures have long indicated, either by direct injunction or by example, that these three disciplines are part of the process of connecting to something bigger than ourselves, to the very force of life that flows through everything and creates all that is. The Queen recognizes that life is being endlessly created in its embodiment as her.

The idea of a spiritual discipline is to make yourself a better vessel for life. For example, detoxing and purifying your body through regular fasting, establishes a more ideal channel for the Divine to enter your body and flourish. In fact, your entire body becomes a more ideal environment. If the idea of fasting appeals to you, you could choose to fast one day a week, once a month, or with whatever frequency suits your own schedule and body. There are different degrees of fasting. It is generally accepted that you won't eat solid foods during the period of the fast. A fast may be complete (water only) or you could choose to ingest juices only or drink only clear liquids. A fast day can extend from one early morning to the next or from dinner to dinner. Whatever best suits you is the best way to do it.

The absence of solid food gives the body a chance to clean itself out through its normal physiological mechanisms and to do some necessary internal repair, which is sometimes put off or happens more slowly when there is food in the belly that still needs to be digested. So, in a sense, when you're fasting you are giving your body a brief break from its cycle of digesting food, expelling waste, and forwarding nutrients throughout the body. When the body has energy to spare, it makes necessary repairs to itself, allows the body to eliminate more waste thoroughly, and allows the digestive system to have some time off.

Another benefit of fasting from food is that it brings to the surface whatever we've been using the food to suppress. Emotional eating is common. In my own life, I remember shortly after my first husband died I was working at a non-profit agency serving people with HIV/AIDS and coming home at night to my own grief. The combination of these stressors led me to look for ways to numb these overwhelming feelings by eating more sugar and drinking a bit more alcohol than was healthy for me. Of course, I started putting on a weight and feeling less healthy. I also did not feel very good about myself and my motivation became weaker. I became less of an ideal vessel for the Queen energy and because of this was less effective in my life. As I worked through my grief and found a different job that was not as draining as the one I had held, my emotional eating lessened. I returned to being a welcoming vessel for the Queen energy. Experts acknowledge that stopping eating sugar alters the way the brain and nervous system function and, I suspect, it makes it easier to open to the Divine.

Caution: A woman should not do an extreme fast if she is underweight, pregnant, nursing, or ill. Restricted eating may be detrimental to your metabolism. Follow the advice of your health care provider as it pertains to your circumstances.

The second technique for creating more ideal conditions within you to connect to your higher self and the Divine is meditation. I like to think of meditation as a fast for the mind. By setting aside ten to thirty minutes every day where you limit your awareness of the unceasing sensory input that accompanies wakefulness helps your mind reset and rest.

Use any of the chakra meditations you have learned in this book. Or sit in a quiet, darkened room and focus on your breathing. There is no one right way to meditate. Just do it on a regular basis and watch the changes it will bring. If you need support to meditate regularly, consider taking a class. There are numerous meditation classes available in most communities. If you cannot get to a class or prefer to meditate alone, YouTube has dozens of guided meditation videos to choose among, many with music, to help you achieve a relaxed, meditative state.

You may have noticed that fasting and meditation are stage setters for us to connect with the Divine—however we personally conceive of it. Having prepared a welcoming mind and body through meditation and gentle fasting, we are poised to issue the invitation to Spirit to bless us with its presence, and that invitation is prayer. Prayer is the third technique used around the world to connect with Life, God, or Source.

As with meditation, prayer is a very personal activity. Nobody can tell you exactly what the experience will be like for you or what the right way to pray is—it is an intentional state of being that may or may not be accompanied by words. In connection with the seventh chakra, you may want your prayer to be a sincere request to become more aware of how the Divine is present in your life or how it can become more present. With this sincere entreaty, you can be assured of its happening.

Once you have opened a channel for a higher power, you may

start feeling more connected to everything you perceive. For instance, you may notice more synchronicities in your daily life. You may find that you are thinking in a less polarized way, seeing that nothing as all right or all wrong. By appreciating the gray areas and multiple points of view, your understanding and tolerance of others may increase.

There are endless ways in which a well-functioning crown chakra, buoyed up by fasting, meditation, and prayer, can add to your being a woman living within the Queen archetype.

For example:

- It will give you mental clarity.
- It will help you recognize the presence of a divine source in your life.
- It will complete and reflect that sense of connection that began in the first chakra, but this time the connection is on a higher level. You now recognize that not only are you connected to your family group, but that you are connected to everything.
- You will see divine grace in your life and feel the comfort of knowing that the Universe has your back.

Transcendence and Universality

The seventh chakra is a door of universal energy and consciousness. Through it, the Queen can reach a higher state of awareness. *Sahasrara* leads beyond materialism to an awareness of the true nature of life, which is abundant in joy, purpose, and curiosity. According to many spiritual teachers, developing higher awareness is either a sudden, spontaneous event or it is a process that can take years to unfold. The catalyst for your awakening may be guidance from an outside source, such as a teacher, but during this process you will ultimately find and follow your inner direction.

It is my belief that what psychologist Carl Jung called the *transcendent function* of the human mind resides in the crown chakra. Following is a workable definition of the transcendent function that is sufficient for our purposes here, with apologies to any Jungian scholars who may be reading this who find it too brief.

Both Carl Jung and Sigmund Freud focused their psychology on the study of the unconscious mind. Freud felt the unconscious was the realm of rejected or repressed material and less than conscious sexual feelings, while Jung believed the unconscious contained all that, as well as a form of mysterious intelligence that compensates for, supports, and even opposes consciousness. To adequately explain this last assertion, Jung had to describe how this opposition could take place. He saw it as a dialogue between the conscious and unconscious, out of which a new direction emerges. It is as if a new being were born from the union of the conscious and unconscious, not, as would be expected, a mingling of the two. Instead of producing a marriage, the transcendent function produces the newborn babe, a new entity. That new entity may be a new awareness of an alternative possibility or a new way of thought about a subject.

Mariah, a single woman in her early fifties, has worked on her spiritual development since her early twenties. In her twenties, as she explored her divine connection, she was attracted to many spiritual teachers. She listened to, or read avidly of their teachings, and tried many of their prescribed practices, following their directions explicitly, without gaining the answers to her many questions. She continued to explore their ways of finding the Divine in her life for a good many years. She often sought validation of her spiritual practices from some of the other followers she met at various workshops and classes but was always left feeling doubtful of whether she was making any spiritual progress.

Many of Mariah's spiritual teachers were truly focused on helping others, but some of her teachers left Mariah feeling empty, powerless, and afraid to step outside their carefully constructed belief systems, or to trust her personal insights. These mostly male leaders were charismatic and presented their ideas with a certainty that was hard to challenge. If someone did, the challenge was often dismissed by the group as a sign of "immature spirituality." The more Mariah searched, the more she compared her spirituality to that of others, the less connected she felt to the Divine. She came to believe that she could not connect without a teacher serving as an intermediary for her. She wanted to "mature" spiritually, but her teacher's views on many things didn't make sense to her.

At one point she began to feel a pervasive sense of isolation from the people in a meditation group she regularly attended. Along with this, Mariah was experiencing frequent headaches and a kind of mental fogginess. This was not how she had imagined her spiritual journey would go!

After a meeting of the meditation group, Mariah found herself talking to a man she didn't know well since he only attended their meetings occasionally. Michael, in the infrequent times she had seen him, had always impressed her because of a strong feeling of serenity that surrounded him. In her mind, he seemed to have it together spiritually, in a way that she felt she was lacking.

Mariah began to ask Michael questions about his personal beliefs and practices. With each question, he answered with few details of his own experience, and skillfully turned the questions back on Mariah, eliciting her responses instead. She had a hard time forming her own answers to her questions, but Michael encouraged her to continue talking about her own spirituality. At one point in their conversation, he commented that she seemed to be looking outside herself for her answers, when she had the ability to find those answers internally.

At first Mariah rejected the idea that she could think these things through on her own or was capable of direct connection with God, but as she pondered the idea and her simultaneous rejection of it, she decided to hold the two opposing ideas in mind and allow them to transform as they would. She "held the tension of the opposites," as this psychological state is often called. This allowed space for something new to happen.

As she and Michael sat together in silence, her mind suddenly cleared, and she recognized that the feelings she was having were byproducts of her own divine connection. The experience was not a pale reproduction of someone else's. What happened for Mariah is an example of the transcendent function at work.

A woman who embodies the Queen knows that if she sits with a tension of the opposites, she often will be gifted with a transcendent perspective that lifts her above her confusion. She trusts the process, knowing that the situation will eventually resolve and accords it the patience it may take. She does not equate speed of resolution with success and does not see time needed for resolution as an indication of faultiness or failure.

Since, by our earlier definition, holding the tension of the opposites and allowing the transcendent function to manifest, is working at that higher level which is the hallmark of the Queen energy.

The Disempowered Queen vs. the Empowered Queen

The disempowered Queen sees herself as defined by qualities outside of herself, such as age, color, sex, financial, and professional status. She discounts anything she cannot perceive with her five senses. Nothing in her life comes to her without her making it happen or working for it. Because she works so hard on this level, she will have achieved a certain amount of success and that, in itself, proves to her that she is totally responsible for her own life and everything in it. She leaves no room for divine grace, if she even knows of it or believes in its existence.

The empowered Queen recognizes that her inspirations come from a developed spiritual life and realizes that she is part of a greater whole. While she is aware that her impetus may be necessary to start or make things happen, she knows she has access to much more than just her own efforts. She trusts that a higher power is guiding and helping her as needed. She sees herself as the initiator of her own growth, but also trusts that beneficial outcomes do not necessarily come only from her own efforts. When her mind is feeling conflicted, she knows how to stay in the moment, perhaps through meditation, and to find the patience to wait for the transcendent function of her psyche to appear and resolve her confusion, wholly believing it will. Her spiritual life provides a home for her soul to reside within her. She has a divine connection, to a sacred or higher aspect of herself. She recognizes there is an intelligence far greater than her own, and trusts that there is a plan of which she may know little; just by being aware of and having worked with divine grace in the past she feels assured that all will be well.

If you take nothing else away from this chapter, I hope you can fully embrace the idea that you don't have to do it alone. The understanding of your partnership with the Divine helps to provide a sense of grace, a valuable quality in a queen. Also, this knowledge allows you to have the ability to rise above your situation. The seventh chakra also helps us get in touch with and employ those most powerful tools—prayer, fasting and meditation. If you haven't yet incorporated these spiritual practices, here is your golden opportunity to see how these ancient and widespread practices can add immeasurably to your life.

Signs Your Seventh Chakra May Be Out of Balance

Your seventh chakra may be out of balance if it is blocked or overactive. This chakra physically affects the area from the top of the ears to the crown of the head. These disturbances may be such things as migraine headaches, neurological disorders, or problems with the pituitary or pineal glands. On an emotional/spiritual level, you may experience frequent bouts of depression and find it difficult to connect with people, resulting in a sense of loneliness or isolation. There may also be a lack of empathy.

An overactive seventh chakra may also cause a sensitivity to light, seizures, confusion, and dizziness.

Meeting the Queen in Your Seventh Chakra

As you did when exploring the previous chakras, if you would like to meet the Queen in your seventh chakra you may invite her to come through you as you go about your daily activities. Also, you may write in your Queen's journal and meditate upon who she is for you. Who are you when you embody her? Take all the time you need or want to experiment with your journaling and meditation about the Queen's seventh chakra aspects. This is the final chakra we will be exploring together in this book.

Inviting the Queen to Come Through You

To experience yourself as a seventh chakra Queen, consciously engage your higher self as you go about your day. You might do this by internally dialoguing with it. This would be particularly useful if you felt as if you were pushing to accomplish tasks and wanted more ease, more flow, more assistance from the universe. It would also be helpful to invite the Queen to inhabit you if you wanted support in overcoming health issues related to the seventh chakra, such as depression or high blood pressure.

As you engage in creative visualization about the Queen archetype, breathe into the area of your seventh chakra and invite her to enter your body. Try imagining what it would feel like to experience internal connectedness in response to any situation you are presently experiencing. See yourself thinking about the situation and going over all the already examined solutions or options, and then imagine your seventh chakra Queen helping you connect to the Divine and magically ramping up so that you are given clarity and an out-of-the-box way to approach your issue.

Journaling About the Queen

You will need paper and a pen to complete this exercise. Or you can park yourself in front of your laptop. Just be sure you are comfortably seated and somewhere you won't be interrupted.

As you did for the first chakra journaling exercise (see page 52), begin by thinking of any situation in your life where you would like to see your own seventh chakra qualities enhanced, such as your connection to Source or a better connection with others in your life. When you find the issue that you'd like to focus on, take some time to reacquaint yourself with what you already know about this issue. From there it should be easy to formulate your question and write it down. Ask the Queen to help you find a better solution by expanding the parameters of your thinking.

After making your request for expanded thinking, ask the Queen to show herself to you in your mind's eye. What do you see first about her today? Flesh out her image. See her in detail. What is she wearing? Perhaps somewhere in her clothing you will see a beautiful violet or white. These are the colors associated with this chakra.

What does her crown look like? Perhaps in this visualization she is wearing a crystal crown, inset with amethysts, since both crystal and amethyst are associated with this chakra.

Mentally ask the Queen to help you clarify her image. Feel her presence growing stronger within you and feel a sense of clarity as she makes her presence palpable. Embody her. Once the image and her presence are clear, hold this perspective and sensation for as long as you can.

Go back to looking at your situation and review it as the Queen. If you are following the instructions written above, you will begin to feel your focus changing and answers becoming clearer and helping you realize how easily you can sense your connection to your higher self. Once this divine connection is foremost in your awareness the words you intend to write in your journal will come easily.

When you feel you have clarity on the seventh chakra issue, open your eyes and write in your journal. Describe everything you saw, heard, felt, and understood. Write in a stream of consciousness without censorship. Let the Queen speak on the page if she wants to.

Relax, if you do not get the answers or the insight you seek immediately. You may need to allow time: you might, in fact, need to wait hours, days, or even weeks. Furthermore, the answer that comes (when it finally does) might not come in the expected way. Be alert to your dreams: answers often show up here. Also, so-called stray thoughts may show up. Before waving them off like buzzing insects, take a curious look to see if your answer is coming to you in these ways. Review this part of your journal frequently, to consciously remember each of the issues you are working on from the perspective of your seventh chakra.

Seventh Chakra Meditation

A third powerful way to invite the Queen into you through your seventh chakra is through meditation. As has already been discussed, meditation has a place of prominence when working with your crown chakra.

For your convenience, I am repeating the following relaxation induction instructions as they appeared in the earlier chakra chapters.

Begin by finding a quiet place where you won't be disturbed for about ten or fifteen minutes. Turn off your cell phone or better yet leave it outside. Make yourself comfortable either in a chair or lying down. It is best if you are sitting to find a chair that supports your spine in an upright position. (This facilitates the movement of the energy.) You may want to cover yourself with a light blanket or throw. Turn the lights down or off. You want to create a comfortable, quiet space where you are not likely to be disturbed.

Close your eyes and take a deep breath. Breathe in as deeply as you can, inhaling through the nose and exhaling through the mouth. Do this for four or five breaths and then begin to exhale through the nose. Continue to think about your breathing in and out through the nose until you start to feel yourself relax. To deepen your sense of relaxation, concentrate on your feet. Notice if they feel achy or tense. With your next inhalation, imagine you are sending a feeling of softness and warmth all the way down to your feet and toes. Send

140

your breath to your feet several times if you wish.

Then, when you are ready with the next inhalation, imagine you are sending the breath down to your lower legs, feeling them being covered with a warm sensation. Feel the tension in your calves let go and sense them becoming softer and less rigid. Bring that warmth up into your thighs, feeling those powerful quads and hamstring muscles let go and relax. Again, when you are ready, allow that soft, caressing warmth to move up into your lower torso, both front and back, as you feel the tension leaving your lower abdomen, your buttocks, and lower back.

Take a moment to really enjoy the feelings of warmth and relaxation. Then feel the warmth spread further up your body to the chest and the mid-back, loosening any tightness that you find there. Focus again for a moment on your breathing as your chest relaxes more and your breathing becomes easier and deeper. Now bring the soft warmth all the way up your torso, all the way to your shoulders.

After a moment or two, check back on your body. It should feel much more relaxed than when you started. If you notice a place (or two) that still feels tense, send your next outbreath to that (or those) spots.

When you feel that you have reached a good state of relaxation begin to imagine the warmth moving up your neck, both front and back, loosening those neck muscles which often hold a great deal of tension. You may want to take some extra time here if you find a lot of tension.

Allow the warmth now to move up the back of your head, covering your entire skull. I often imagine this feeling like a baby's bonnet. Let the warmth then begin to travel down your forehead, smoothing and soothing it. The warmth can then move further down your face all the way to the jawline.

Now, as you are feeling very relaxed, ask the Queen to appear to you in your mind's eye. Since we are in the seventh chakra you may see her with rays of light surrounding her, or with some other indicator of her connection to source.

As mentioned before, you may see her wearing a beautiful violet colored robe, the color associated with *sahasrara*. Her crown could be crystal. At her feet would be symbols of the gifts she brings from the seventh chakra such as a lotus flower, which is the symbol of the crown chakra, showing us an incredibly beautiful, fragrant flower that grows from having its feet in the mud. You may want to use this or any symbol that speaks to you of the Divine.

This is your meditation, so feel free to imagine the Queen in the way that most reflects who you are. Take time to embellish your vision of her adding whatever details seem to belong. As you do this, your seventh chakra Queen will become more alive to you.

Now as you continue to hold your vision of her see her beckon to you. See yourself walking toward her as she gently takes your hand. Ask her to bless you with her powerful presence and to give you all the qualities she represents. See her putting her hand on the top of your head and feel the strength of her energy enter you. Take a moment with this letting yourself really *feel* it. Let that seventh chakra energy of the Queen move down and flow through your whole body all the way down to your feet.

See your Queen with connections to all that is. Take a minute or two to let this happen. When the visualization feels complete allow the image to fade as you thank your Queen for her blessings and support.

As you continue with your deep breathing feel yourself returning to your everyday awareness and when you are ready open your eyes and rub the palms of your hands and the soles of your feet together to bring yourself fully back into physical reality. When you feel fully present in your body you may return to your daily activities knowing that you have done something wonderful and healing for yourself.

Summary
The Queen in the Seventh Chakra

Below is a short list of the ways in which you can remind yourself of how the seventh chakra looks in a woman who embodies the Queen.

The Queen:

- Looks for help from known and unknown sources. She trusts that a higher power is guiding and helping her, as needed.
- Sees herself as the initiator of her own growth but trusts that beneficial outcomes do not necessarily come only from her own efforts.
- Recognizes that her inspirations come from a developed spiritual life.
- Provides a home for her soul to reside within her.
- Is able to wait for the "transcendent function" to appear, wholly believing it will.

CHAPTER 10

INVITING THE QUEEN THROUGH RITUAL

Designing and performing a ritual, either by yourself or in the company of close friends and family, is a powerful way of inviting the energy of the Queen to manifest in your life. Below you will find some basic information about rituals to help you design and conduct a self-coronation. Because you are the Queen, only you have the power to claim this status by crowning yourself. Just remember that this is a *personal ritual*.

Ritual

Rituals are a prescribed series of words and actions designed to bring importance and attention to their subject by taking those words and actions out of their everyday context and marking them out as special moments that have meaning. If witnessed by others in addition to the celebrant (the woman conducting the ritual), the ritual informs those present that something special is occurring. By bringing importance and attention to what is framed within the ritual, a greater importance is lent to the content, sometimes raising it to the level of the numinous, or sacred. In this way, the minds and hearts of the participants and celebrant will consider the ritual to be set apart from everyday life, ordinary time, and set in sacred time.

You will want to make your coronation ritual personal in every way you can. Incorporating objects, words, music, and poetry that have a heartfelt connection increases how deeply you will take in the energy and ideas invoked in the ritual. There are no other specific rules to follow. Nothing you do could ever invalidate a ritual you yourself design.

Rituals have been used throughout recorded history, and most likely, well before that. They often contain recognizable elements such as: cleansing, grounding, creating a sacred space, calling upon the powers of the elements and directions, invoking a deity, the "working," the raising and releasing of power, and finally, a centering or meditation.

The steps of a Queen ritual may look something like the following.

Preparation

Ahead of time, assemble various objects you plan to use in the Working of your ritual (see below). You might, for example, gather objects like a crown (definitely), a scepter, a goddess statue, and a picture of a woman who symbolizes the Queen to you.

You may also wish to establish and decorate a ritual table or altar with cloths of your favorite color and things that have meaning for you, which reflect both the life you have led thus far and symbolize your hopes for your future. Baby cups could symbolize your children, wedding rings, your spouse. Also consider crystals, flowers, candles, and even jewelry.

Red and purple are good choices of color for Queen rituals. According to color experts, red represents blood, fire, passion, strength, power, and courage. It is an intense color that boosts the metabolism, increasing perspiration and raising blood pressure. Purple, which combines red and blue, is associated with royalty. Rare in nature, most people find it pleasing. Historically in western culture, it symbolizes nobility, dignity, wisdom, luxury, independence, and magic.

Cleansing

You may take a bath or smudge your body and space with the smoke of burning sage, the spritzing of holy water, or doing any other cleansing act that appeals to you.

Grounding

It's recommended to do something to help you and other participants become totally present to what is about to unfold. This could be a guided meditation, read aloud by you or another celebrant, that helps you and your guests to be fully present in your bodies; also, to help quiet the noise in the head that Buddhists would call the *monkey mind.*

Creating a Sacred Space

One way to make the space in which the ritual is occurring safe and sacred is by visualizing a protective circle of light around it. Or you may delineate the boundaries of the space by sprinkling a circle with salt or by carrying incense around the circle.

Calling on the Elements and/or the Directions

In Native American spiritual tradition, before doing a ceremony, an invitation is offered to spirits from all corners of the world to bring their energy into the sacred space the celebrant has established. Traditionally, these are the spirits of the East (air), the South (fire), the West (water), the North (earth), and Space (spirit). When this step is completed, you will have built a container for the ritual with a representation of the power of the elements.

Invoking the Queen

Please feel free to issue an invocation in a way that does not run contrary to your own spiritual beliefs (or absence of them). One way would be to invoke the highest vibration of what an evolved Queen might be. Ask her to come to you.

Statement of Purpose of the Ritual

In the context of a coronation, this could be to invite the Queen into your life so that you can manifest all that is in keeping with the archetype.

The Working

This is the very heart of your ritual. As you approach your table or altar, which is covered with articles you assembled during Preparation (see above), you may want to speak to those in attendance, telling them what particular queenly qualities you want to manifest in your life and asking them to reflect on those they similarly may wish to manifest. These qualities may be to become far-seeing, beneficent, and powerful. Other qualities may have to do with the Queen being the conduit to the next generation by teaching the arts of living, or by passing along family traditions and history. You may also want to take this opportunity to make a declaration of your desire to benefit your extended family, the local or extended community, or even the world.

After you have said everything you want, comes the moment of Crowning Yourself Queen.

Crowning Yourself Queen

Taking the crown from its place on the altar, place it upon your own head while saying something like:

I, _____[INSERT YOUR NAME], having recognized my own unique talents and abilities, and having connected with my own feminine divinity, do take this crown for myself. I do this on _____[INSERT DATE], in the presence of my own sister queens, proclaiming myself to be a Queen among Queens. So be it.

Raising and Releasing the Power

The self-crowning and all the preparation steps will have raised the energy in the room. It is now the time to briefly raise it further by an action such as singing, drumming, chanting, or dancing.

When you can no longer hold the energy, consciously release it to the Universe by saying something like: "I now release the power which has held us until now, knowing it will join with All That Is and in time begin to manifest the qualities of the Queen in me."

Centering, Communion, Meditation

After Raising and Releasing the Power, it is now time to sit quietly for a few minutes to allow yourself to become centered. You may pray, meditate, or allow your feelings to emerge. If you are holding a group coronation, each woman should center on her own in silence, respecting the time it takes for the others to feel complete. After the ritual is concluded, participants may enjoy socializing.

Allison had discussed with several of her close friends that she wanted to do a crowning ritual to mark the occasion of her sixtieth birthday. In the past, some of her friends had done croning rituals to celebrate their passage into cronehood. Allison had never felt a connection with the Crone archetype—at least not yet, even as she approached the beginning of her seventh decade. Having recently heard about the Queen archetype, she felt that better defined what she saw for herself now and in the years to come. Allison spent some time talking with her friends about what the Queen archetype symbolized for her. They agreed they would be honored to participate in this crowning ritual for Allison.

Allison and her friends designed a very personal ritual for Allison, using the foregoing ritual outline as their guide. They added a birthday party, with some of Allison's favorite foods and a birthday cake. They invited some other women who were important in Allison's life, like her younger sister, and an old friend from Allison's hometown.

Allison and I spoke a few days after her crowning ritual/birthday and I asked her what had been meaningful to her about this recent event. Allison said that, of course, spending her sixtieth birthday with close women friends and relatives was an important part of the day, and added that the bringing the energy of the Queen so palpably into the room had been unexpectedly powerful. She said the act of proclaiming herself a Queen and putting a crown on her own head had sent chills through her. At that moment, she felt shift in her own energy. She came away from it feeling stronger and more powerful and completely worthy of operating at a higher level. Allison also said that the feelings had persisted during the ensuing days. She also felt that the ritual itself, with its very personal references, had been the catalyst.

EPILOGUE:

MY PROCESS DURING THE WRITING OF THIS BOOK

Fairly early in my adult life, I made the decision not to have children, being involved with and later married to a man who made it clear early in our relationship that he did not intend to be a father. I also felt that my primary job in this life was to mother myself and develop the best of who I was. I was not aware for many years that the experience of becoming a mother to my own children would have honed and shaped me in a way that would rival any self-mothering. So, I remained, and continue to be, childless by choice.

My life unfolded in a way I could not foresee. When in my late sixties and a widow, my long-time best friend died of complications of breast cancer treatment. Her husband, who had been my friend for the twenty-eight years they were married, unexpectedly began to attract me. He acknowledged having feelings for me as well. In a short time, we became a couple and were married three years later. With this new marriage came his three grown children and four grandchildren.

I have known my husband's children for as long as I have known my husband and I am godmother to the youngest. There was no need for me to step into a traditional mother role, but over the years I have become at least some version of a stepmother (not the evil kind, I trust), as well as a step-grandmother.

In light of the work I have done on this book and my contemplation of the feminine archetypes and archetypal energies I was writing about, I realized more and more each day that the psyche/soul attracts what it needs. By choosing not to be a biological mother, I had missed out on some important experiences. But I had other experiences that incorporated mothering energy.

Within the same period as I was writing, I formed a very close bond with my cat, Mr. C, who was diagnosed with hyperthyroidism and several months later began to have intestinal problems. These might have been an outcome of the thyroid problem or a co-occurring issue. There was even a suspicion of cancer. He was placed on a rollercoaster of treatment and medication, at times clearly not feeling well and needing to retreat into a closet. He lost weight and stopped being the sweet kitty I knew. My care of him, giving him twice-daily medications, worrying, taking him in for tests, and so on, affected me in a deep place. I found myself feeling in a very empathic way what it must be like to be the mother of a chronically ill child. I have realized how this powerful, ever-present concern for another creature who is dependent on your care colors every aspect of your waking day. If the being under your care (in my case, a sick cat) has a good day, your day is good. Boundaries get bent and the being's needs become paramount. Feels like Mother archetypal energy to me.

Meanwhile back on the human relations side—my step-daughters' responses to my becoming part of their family were each different. The two older daughters were accepting and approving. The youngest daughter, the child of my late friend, had a harder time accepting any one who would seem to be "taking her mother's place." I therefore made a very conscious effort not to try to seem like I was playing Mom, at times perhaps going too far the other way. After six years of walking the tightrope and monitoring my own feelings about what I see as my role, and during the writing of this book, we arrived at a happy place.

My youngest step-daughter has done the personal work which was always only hers to do, and I also have done mine. The outcome was that she asked me to help plan her wedding, saying that I am the closest thing to a mother that she has, thereby triggering feelings of kinship that I hadn't known were there.

As I said before, the psyche knows what it needs and attracts it to itself!

This is also how it will be for you as you continue to explore the archetype of the Queen. If you feel there is a part of your development that has been lacking in the archetypal realms of Maiden or Mother, you might like to look over the following few questions to help you pinpoint it more surely. Your answers will, of course, bring you the conscious awareness you seek, and that awareness will begin to attract the corrective experiences you need.

Questions to Ponder

In thinking about your journey through your life thus far, have any of the stages of feminine development not been fully available to you, or not fully experienced? (We really are only talking about the Maiden and the Mother, since the stage of Crone follows the stage of Queen.)

- When you were a young, single woman, did you get the opportunity to engage your sense of adventure and self-sufficiency that are often hallmarks of the Maiden?
- Did you get to fully recognize and enjoy your own burgeoning sexuality?
- Did adolescent sexual adventures cause problems for you?
- Was your sexuality repressed?
- If you felt drawn to nature, were you able to experience it sufficiently, or were unable to spend time in nature or with animals?
- Were you in some way aware of being "one unto herself"?

ACKNOWLEDGEMENTS

There are so many people I want to acknowledge who helped in the creation of this book, and it seems to me that listing them in the chronological order of each person's support makes about as much sense as any other way of listing them.

One of my earliest supporters and collaborators is Patricia Ariadne, Ph.D., whose interest in this subject and unwavering vision for all that it might be helped me begin, and encouraged me throughout the process. Since she had already written and published four books of her own, she gave me hope that I could do this, too.

Stephanie Gunning, my editor, who spent nearly a year helping me flesh out the Queen and making her accessible to the readers, was my teacher, coach and cheerleader. I am so happy I had an editor who already knew the Queen in her heart.

I would like to acknowledge my friends, Mary Ellen Krut and Tina Howard who read an early version of the manuscript with attention and made so many good suggestions. Also, I would like to include Rachel Weinstock, my social media maven, who has helped me spread the word of the Queen even before the book was published. And thanks to Shaila Abdullah, my web designer, who created the beautiful red artwork which now adorns the cover.

I would also like to acknowledge my publisher, Jennifer Leigh Selig, of Mandorla Books, for her unerring understanding of Archetypal Psychology and Jungian thought, assuring me of explaining these often complex concepts in an accurate manner.

Finally, I would like to acknowledge my husband, Larry, who bore the brunt of my long "confinement" with *Inviting the Queen*, and was always supportive, patient and encouraging.

RESOURCES

Now that you've been introduced to the Queen and have begun to experience what it feels like to embody her energy in your own life, you may wish to go deeper with your exploration. I will be creating the following programs to give you greater support than you can get from a book alone.

You may check my website www.sandrarogerslmft.com, for updated information on the Inviting the Queen Seminar, Inviting the Queen Personal Coaching, Inviting the Queen Meditation Audio, Inviting the Queen Online Course, and Inviting the Queen workshops. If you would like to have a workshop presented to your group, please contact me at srogerslmft@gmail.com.

Keirsey Temperament Sorter available online at www.keirsey.com.

ABOUT THE AUTHOR

Sandra Rogers, M.A., LMFT, is a licensed marriage and family therapist in private practice, specializing in object relations and transpersonal psychotherapy. Schooled in the depth psychology of Carl Jung and the archetypal psychology of James Hillman at Pacifica Graduate Institute in Santa Barbara, California, she believes that self-knowledge, including an awareness of the personal unconscious, opens the door to living an effective, authentic life. She often uses dream work, clinical hypnosis, guided imagery, and art therapy to help deepen the work. She believes that by helping her clients find their strengths and unique qualities they can become more self-aware and access their own inner wisdom, heal where they need to, and reach their goals.

The idea of the Queen archetype sprang from her long-held interest in the Crone archetype, which she found most mid-life women strongly rejected.

Sandra lives with her husband, Larry, in the Southern California beach town of Encinitas.

BOOK CLUB DISCUSSION SUGGESTIONS

1. What aspects of the concept of the Queen, both as a life stage and an archetype, speak to you?
2. What did you find interesting about the idea of archetypes? What questions may have arisen about them?
3. How do you imagine the archetypal energy of the Queen could enhance your life at midlife and beyond? How has she already done so, if you're knee-deep in that stage?
4. Who are the Queens in your life, both past and present? What qualities do they embody? What lessons have you learned from them?
5. What examples from the book did you find most resonant with your own life journey? Most dissonant?
6. Looking at your journey in midlife and beyond through the chakra system, which stage do you find yourself in now? How are you navigating it?
7. If you've been through earlier stages of the chakras, share examples of how you embodied the Queen in each of the stages.
8. Don't be afraid to discuss the embodied Queen versus the disembodied Queen. How has the latter shown up in your journey? In what stages of the journey have you been most disembodied?
9. If you did the exercises (i.e., journaling, meditation, active imagination), share a particular discovery that surprised you.
10. If you performed a self-coronation ritual, describe your experience. If you did not do one yet, would every woman in your club commit to trying one, and coming back and sharing results at your next meeting?

Made in United States
Troutdale, OR
09/22/2023

13115878R00096